SECTEU

1962

1968

HIS CRITICAL MIRROR

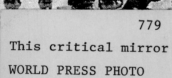

1974

1975

THIS CRITICAL MIRROR

For forty years the World Press Photo Foundation has offered a contemporary mirror to history as it unfolds. As the millennium approaches there is an opportunity to reflect on the second half of the twentieth century and the World Press Photo is uniquely placed to compile a review of these decades and the imagery that will shape the next century.

40 YEARS OF WORLD PRESS PHOTO

"Culture saves nothing or nobody, nor does it justify. But it is a product of man:

Sartre (Words, part 2)

he projects himself through it: this critical mirror alone shows him his image."

Edited by **Stephen Mayes**

Foreword by **Sebastião Salgado**

Thames and Hudson

CONTENTS

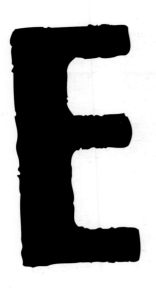

Sebastião Salgado

The sum of the pictures taken since 1956 and preserved in the archives of the World Press Photo Foundation - important pictures, dramatic and occasionally pathetic - reconstructs part of the history of the world over four decades. They raise relevant questions, both simple and obvious, in the minds of those who view them. When a photographer covers "hot" news, in the company of many of his colleagues from the written press, from radio and from television, questions will arise, such as: why is he here? Is he on assignment? For whom? For my part, I believe he reacts, often instinctively, to the pressures of a period in history. We photographers all serve, each in our own way, as links to different parts of the world. Our work leads us to places where others cannot go in order to show what others would otherwise not be able to see. A reporter doesn't create the incident, as is sometimes intimated; he is the "critical mirror".

Unlike television journalists, press photographers do not work as a team; we face the event alone. Everything which constitutes a person joins in that process which produces a photograph. Like all humans, we are a curious mixture; we are bearers of an ideology and a personal history that blends in the events and subjects our cameras focus on. We become in our turn the fruit of our work. Showing others our photographs is a kind of rebirth for us.
The photographer, whether he be called a press photographer, a photojournalist, a documentary or a socially concerned photographer, acts not as a voyeur but as an interpellator. His work is not conclusive in itself, but it is a reflection. This is his way of acting on the event. His pictures often put the facts, the world and all of us, to account. He takes the temperature of our world.
He knows he will resolve nothing, but certain pictures can help to provoke a debate and influence the way the world works.

The example of the Vietnam war always comes to mind because it is so revealing. What we recall with hindsight, are photographs rather than moving images. It is these "decisive moments", these fateful seconds, that have now become part of our collective memory. Such pictures and most of the ones gathered together in this collection emphasize the need to search out such situations. If they are harsh, atrocious, sometimes unbearable, it is our world that generated them; it is the world's violence that they bring home to us. We can never see enough of them. Unlike others, I feel, for example, that we have not seen enough documentation of what has happened in Africa in the last few years. We should not hesitate to continue to show photographs of the genocide in Rwanda. They should enable all the players in this drama to exorcise what happened and to rebuild and find the way to a solution, so that such atrocities are never repeated. Not a single being on earth should be spared these pictures. This applies likewise to Bosnia and Chechnya. It is vital that everyone sees them and recognizes themselves, otherwise the human species, which is both responsible for and the victim of these horrors, may one day disappear completely.

I am proud to be part of this small world of photographers who piece together the very soul of our society. The miracle of photography, of pictures in general, is that they can be transmitted to everyone without the need for translation. They are the purest expression of humanity, its universal language and its critical mirror. We must not try to escape from this reflection. We must accept it and respect it, so that we can take part in the evolution of society, and its process of change.

INTR ODUCTION

1

Howard Chapnick

Observations on
photojournalism in
the second half of
the 20th century

For forty years, the World Press Photo Foundation has offered a contemporary mirror to history, a mirror of diversity serving as a visual biography of the past, a history of the moment, and a compilation of events that shape the future. That this should occur simultaneously with the millennium and the dawning of the information age is fortuitous because it serves as a defining demarcation in the visual recording of man´s rite of passage on earth. William Ivins, former Curator of Prints and Drawings at the Metropolitan Museum, New York City, said that the nineteenth century began by believing that what was reasonable was true and it ended up believing that what it saw photographed was true. The twentieth century ends by questioning the very authenticity of every image that can now be subjected to the undetected alteration of sophisticated technology. At hostage is the delicate concept of truth. Is it absolute? Is it subjective? Is it flexible and amorphous?

The roots of commercial, advertising and art photography are based on philosophical truths, not nurtured by reality. Such photography can draw on the creativity of the mind and camera and lens technologies to alter, deface, manipulate, distort, or romanticize without penalty to the purity of the work. At risk is the artist´s judgement in the conceptualization of an idea and in bringing it to full flower.

The integrity and purity of press photography and photojournalism are inviolable. The fountainhead of journalistic photography is its testament to truth. Therefore, the elements in a news or journalistic photograph cannot be moved, reordered, reconstructed, directed, manipulated, or managed. The journalistic photographer photographs what is, not what was, or what might have been.

2

3

Does journalistic integrity demand objectivity? Can a photojournalist be a passionate protagonist for a specific point of view? If one believes as I do that objectivity is an elusive grail, one has to embrace a philosophy that ascribes subjective concerns to social and political issues. The history of photography is replete with stories where the photographer´s concerns have been translated into powerful movements to repair the social fabric, enhance the environment or affect political stability. Photographic historians proudly look back to the work of Lewis Hine and Jacob Riis who fought against child labour and sweatshops; to Roy Stryker´s Farm Security Agency photographers who helped America overcome an insidious economic depression; and to William Henry Jackson, whose missionary scenic photographs helped to establish and preserve America´s National Park System.

1 **Dorothea Lange**
USA
Migrant Mother
NIPOMA CALIFORNIA 1936

2 **Donna Ferrato**
USA
Domestic Violence
USA 1991

3 **Lewis W. Hine**
USA
Child in Carolina Cotton Mill
USA 1908

4 **William H. Jackson**
USA
Tower Falls
YELLOWSTONE USA 1872

4

Although these examples predate the establishment of World Press Photo Foundation, the photojournalists of the last forty years have unselfconsciously chosen to build a tradition of proactive, socially-driven, idealistic press photography that attempts to change the world. In this subject matter is the stuff of life, the journalist´s attempts to explain man to himself, to present the obscene, to neglect the trivial in search of the profound.

What is remarkable is that in these forty years either the world has changed or photographers have revealed layers of society that never before existed. War photography, first represented by static and sanitized Crimean War photographs, has been transformed into dynamic 'in your face' photography that comes ever closer to moments of death in Korea, Vietnam and Yugoslavia. The hygienic viewpoint of World War II that disallowed the publication of dead bodies was replaced by bloody battlefields served with evening dinner and television news. Nevertheless, the world press continues to reflect the hot spot of the week, moving its nomadic hordes of photographic and word journalists to deep-seated ethnic, political, racial and religious strife on every continent in the world.

Ever more sophisticated and better educated photojournalists turned their cameras to explore the worlds of drugs (Eugene Richards) and domestic violence (Donna Ferrato). Politically, photographers have successfully challenged authoritarian and repressive governments, such as Charles Moore of the Birmingham Riots and David Turnley´s equally courageous efforts to combat apartheid in South Africa. What defeated the massive American armed forces in Vietnam? An American public whose visual consciousness had been penetrated by Life Magazine´s publication of the faces of 107 GIs who died during a representative week, Eddie Adams' photograph of the suspected North Vietnam officer being killed point-blank by General Loan and Nick Ut´s picture of the screaming naked napalmed girl along the road. The cumulative effect of these and other images like John Filo´s Kent State Massacre helped to destroy the American will to invest further in a war of attrition that had already stimulated an American generation schism built on a powerful anti-war movement. Testament to the power of photography was the role it played in aiding and documenting the ultimate breakdown of Soviet style communism in Europe and the evershifting sands of the fragile peace that lay over the national movements of Palestine, Ireland and China.

These critical years will also be remembered for the groundbreaking work that humanized environmental threats to our well-being. W. Eugene Smith´s Minamata coverage personalized the human impact of mercury poisoning on a fishing village in Japan as did Bartholomew´s documentation of Bhopal calling to account the industrial accident of a neglectful company that resulted in death and thousands of cases of blindness. And a high point of world photojournalism may have been to stimulate the outpouring of aid for the tragic victims of famine in the Sahel and Somalia.

The publication of international press photography is dependent on the coming together of a loose alliance of creative staff photographers, freelance photographers, photographic agencies, and magazines. Each week´s distillation of great press photography is filtered through this network to produce a diary marking man´s existence on earth, impacted by natural disasters, conditioned by sociological concerns and affected by man´s vision. What emerges is an astonishing compilation of incredibly complex imagery seen almost simultaneously by billions of people. Each year, when the call for entries to the World Press Photo contest goes out, the visual history of that year falls into place. Forty years later, we have the unique opportunity to honour those photographers who have covered the cataclysmic events that have shaped our times. These twentieth century nomads have constructed for us a bridge to better understanding of this complicated, interdependent world. We pause to contemplate finite fractions of time: silent they speak and motionless they move. The efforts of these photographers enrich journalism, enhance knowledge, and ennoble our profession.

FROM THE WORLD PR

DAVID GOLDBLATT
THE HUMAN SPIRIT AND
THE PHOTOGRAPH
ON PHOTOGRAPHING THE
INVISIBLE SUBJECT

5

David Goldblatt

*The Human Spirit
and the Photograph*

*On photographing
the invisible subject*

How is spirit revealed in a photograph? Of necessity photographs can show only those aspects of people that we can see and touch: the body, the body clothed and unclothed, the body's exterior and its interior - whether exposed by violence, surgery, or x-rays - but always and only the body. Thoughts, emotions, psyche, spirit, are themselves invisible and beyond the reach of our camera. However, we can infer them from photographs.

Growing up, we learn through social interaction that other people have emotions, thoughts, feelings, spirit, not unlike our own. We communicate these verbally through language and non-verbally through our awareness of other people's bodies. We scan each other's eyes, mouth, face, the tensing of muscles, the movement of limbs for signs of what the other is 'really' thinking or feeling; for clues to the nature of their spirit. It is this learnt ability to read each other that we bring to photographs.

5 **David C. Turnley**
USA
*US Sergeant Ken
Kozakiewicz cries as he
learns that the body bag,
next to him in the medical
evacuation helicopter,
contains the body of his
friend killed by 'friendly fire'*
IRAQ/KUWAIT, 1991

6 **Stuart Franklin**
UK
*Students on the eve
of the uprising in
Tiananmen Square*
BEIJING, CHINA, 1989

Life is an ongoing process: we see the body's
signs changing and evolving as we watch each
other. In photographs the clues are frozen.
This both limits the photograph and at the
same time gives it the possibility of being an
extraordinarily powerful statement about the
human spirit. The limitation is that we can
only know or infer what that single image dis-
closes. The potency of the image lies in the
possibility that being frozen, it can isolate
qualities of spirit not easily discernible in the
flux of life: we can go back to the image again
and again and penetrate to other and often
deeper layers of awareness of spirit. The spiritual qualities are, as it were, stored electricity.
This potential creates an answering tension, a
charge in us, the viewers, which draws us into
the photograph and leads to an interplay
between our own spirit and that which has
been revealed in the photograph.
Consider David Turnley's 1991 photograph of
an American soldier weeping. I search for clues
to his anguish and cannot find them in the
photograph. He cries but it is difficult to cry
with him or for him. Then reading the caption
we learn that he weeps for a friend dead in a
body bag next to him, killed by 'friendly fire'.

Now his anguish takes shape. Here are tears of love and a
sense of the utter futility of a life wasted. But we have
'reached' this man's spirit through the caption, not through
what was implicit in the photograph. The photograph itself is
curiously flat. All photographs, particularly news photographs need captions. But the vital ingredients need to come
from the pictures themselves rather than extraneously, as in
this case, from the captions, which should simply explain.
In contrast, Stuart Franklin's 1989 photograph of the
student uprising on Tiananmen Square is extraordinarily
complete in itself. Not only is the story there in the flags,
the building, the scurrying figures and the heroic young
man, but the photograph is remarkably eloquent of these
youthful spirits in revolt. It encapsulates precisely
Wordsworth's feelings after the French Revolution, "Bliss was
it in that dawn to be alive,/ But to be young was very
heaven!" Yet judging by his face the young man's triumph
seems measured rather than wild, as though he is conscious
of the portentousness of what he is doing. Even in its graceful
strength his naked torso seems unbearably vulnerable; history
showed it to be so.

6

7 **Sebastião Salgado**
BRAZIL
*Famine victims in
a refugee camp*
ETHIOPIA, MARCH, 1984

8 **Ovie Carter**
USA
*Orphaned Saku Barman
at a refugee station*
SINGIMARIE PACHUNIPER
INDIA, 1974

9 **Mary Ellen Mark**
USA
*Fantaye Abay in a
refugee camp in famine-
stricken Ethiopia*
1985

7

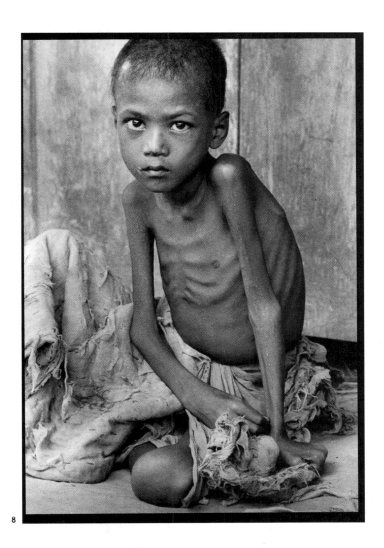

8

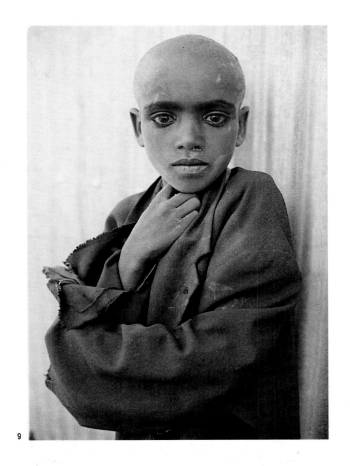

9

A subject that has recurred in much of the World Press Photo archive is the famines that have afflicted Africa and parts of Asia over the last few decades. Starting with Ovie Carter's 1974 photographs and ending with James Nachtwey's of 1992 I counted some twenty-two coverages of this subject in eighteen years. In heart-rending, strongly composed and sometimes almost obscenely beautiful images (for example Sebastiao Salgado's 1984 hooded figures), the horror of starvation is potently conveyed. Yet there is not much evidence of the human spirit in most of this work.

It is as though the photographers saw only the shrivelled bodies, the gaunt faces, the outstretched begging hands.

The people within those bodies, the individual, living, interacting, sentient beings are strangely absent. Starvation notwithstand-ing, even in lassitude and despair, life surely went on and the spirit with it?

With the exception of the work of two photographers there was little to indicate this. In Mary Ellen Mark's 1985 photograph of a malnourished boy something extraordinary happens. We, the viewers seem to take the place of the photographer. We seem to look into the child's eyes and he into ours. In that process we recognize him as a person, an individual. We sense something of his being: fragile yet strong and not without hope. Compare this with the very similar 1974 photograph by Ovie Carter. Carter seems to have looked at the child and the child warily back at him - or probably at his camera. No resonance, no meaningful moment of awareness of each other seems to have occurred between Carter and his subject. The difference between the two photographs is subtle, but while Carter's photograph is an honest and compassionate description of the exterior of things, Mark's penetrates to the spirit.

In Mark's 1985 photograph of a mother, child and doctor, love, tenderness and yearning are subtly conveyed in a complex interweaving of their three bodies, in the strength and support of the hands of the women, in their remarkably eloquent mouths, their lidded eyes and the invisible mouth of the child. Such photographs seldom come easily, the photographer has to work towards them by a sort of empathetic 'tuning in' to the spirit of her subjects.

James Nachtwey did something in the Sudan in 1988 that few press photographers would have dared. Faced with photographing black people under the intense brightness of the overhead African sun on colour film, he refrained from using fill-in flash. The resulting harshness has brutally sculpted hollowed ribcages and heads and conveyed something of the reality of the scratching for food in a scorched land. These are potent photographs about the circumstances of survival. However they do not penetrate beyond the circumstantial.

Nachtwey's 1992 photograph of a woman carrying her dead child to the grave is of quite a different order. We can hardly see the woman's face yet we sense her tender and terrible concentration on the child hidden in its virginal shroud. The concentric folds of her robe seem to speak of her womanliness. The frail burden bears her down, yet she carries it with infinite care. Her powerful feet grip the hard, grassless earth of a rainless Africa in which she seems to be the only living being. Nachtwey has revealed this all without drama, without effects. The camera has been used simply to photograph what was there. This photograph approaches that ineffable quality that might be called profound.

10

10 **Mary Ellen Mark**
USA
*Young refugee boy
embraces doctor during
medical examination*
ETHIOPIA, 1985

11, 13 **James Nachtwey**
USA
*Refugees affected by
famine during the
civil war in Sudan*
1988

12 **James Nachtwey**
USA
*A woman carries her
dead child to the grave*
BARDERA, SOMALIA, 1992

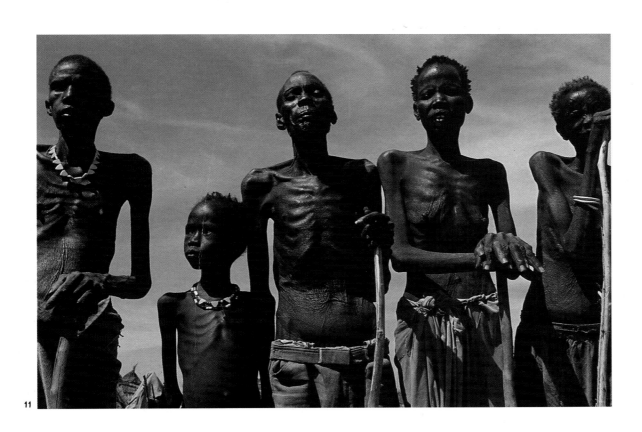

11

12

13

The contemporary context within which many
of these pictures were first seen itself offers a
commentary on the human spirit. In the World
Press Photo Yearbook of 1977 a pretty actress
in a spoof of lifting a car with a man in it
counterpoises with a weightlifter, a legless war
victim exercising with dumb-bells and a Niger
woman with an enormous burden of firewood.
As far as the editors were concerned all of these
people lifted weights; therefore, they were all
equal and comparable. But clearly the spiritual
values revealed in the photographs were not.

World Press Photo Yearbook 1977

14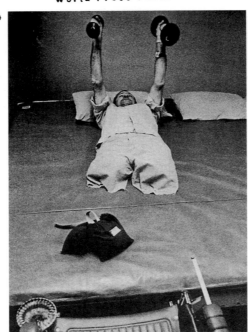

15

16

17

The photograph of the legless man speaks of his courage and determination; the photograph of the wood carrier is an almost archetypal image of the strength and dignity that so many African women bring to a chore that dominates millions of lives on this continent. Both of these photographs are trivialized by their juxtaposition with two that are as trite in their subject matter as they are in their treatment.

Later Yearbooks are less prone to this sort of editorializing. Increasingly they have been designed with sensitivity to the content and meaning of the photographs. Looking through some forty years of the World Press Photo archive it seems too that the photography published has become more powerful in its gripping immediacy. This may have something to do with changes in the way photographers have had to work in order to compete with television - they seem to get ever closer to their subjects.

It may also have to do with improvements in layout, the quality of reproduction and the paper used. I have to say, however, that although these books have become remarkably vivid displays of outstanding editorial photography, the human spirit is often superficially dealt with. What Dorothea Lange called 'second lookers', photographs that you go back to again and again, are rare. But then this should not surprise us: profundity is no less elusive in photography than it is in literature or any other form of communication between humans.

FROM THE WOR

KATHY RYAN
NEWSMAKERS

NEWS IS MADE ABOUT PEOPLE AND
IT IS MADE BY PEOPLE NOT ALL OF THEM
FAMOUS OR POWERFUL

LD PRESS PHOTO ARCHIVE

18

Kathy Ryan
Newsmakers

*News is made
about people and
it is made by
people, not all of
them famous or
powerful*

Imagine for a moment you have entered an unusual house.
You walk down a very long corridor. There are thousands of
rooms on either side. The rooms are filled with people.
Every room, whether crowded with many, or occupied by one,
is bursting with emotion. You recognize many of the people
instantly. Others you are seeing for the first time.
As you proceed the noise varies. Sometimes, it is very, very loud.
Other times there is utter silence. You walk by some rooms
quickly, barely stopping to take a look. At others, you have
difficulty moving on. Your eyes might be held by another
pair of eyes. Or you might stare unobserved. The people in this
place share something. They are all pictured in the pages of
the World Press Photo archives. Some chose to enter their
rooms. Others were cast there by fate. Photojournalists brought
them here. They thought we should see them. They framed
these newsmakers in an instant so they could tell their stories
forever.

The picture of helpless Kim Phuc communicates a hidden message about power. The little girl is powerless, yet the image has enormous power. All eyes fixed on one powerless child, and it was enough to change world affairs. The term 'newsmakers' suggests power on the part of those pictured - as if the people in the coming pages chose to make the news. It did not always happen that way. Kim Phuc did not choose to become an icon of anti-war sentiment any more than she chose to find herself in a napalm storm. She did choose to sit for a portrait recently. Even though one second in the life of Kim Phuc is frozen in an eternal present for the rest of the world, for Kim Phuc time did not stop.

18 Joe McNally
USA
Kim Phuc Phan Thi twenty-three years after the napalm-bombing of her home village in South Vietnam

19 Nick Út
USA
Nine-year old Kim Phuc Phan Thi runs down the road after tearing off her napalm-burned clothing
TRANGBANG, SOUTH VIETNAM
8 JUNE, 1972

War and photojournalism merged
shortly after the discovery of
photography. Since then, the
collaboration has flourished.
An unending number of conflicts
call combat photographers to duty.
It seems, unfortunately, that the
soldier will always be counted
among the 'newsmakers'.
This is a memorable image from
the Vietnam war. The soldier in the
background appears, in his wild
gesture to the heavens, to be
demanding an explanation for all
this madness. His comrades form
a statuesque trio of heroism and
valor as they struggle to bring
their wounded comrade to safety.
The soldier in the foreground
narrates the scene for us, putting
a face on all this suffering.
These men have wandered
into hell.
As with all good journalism, the
photo also does duty as a factual
document. The man in the background is calling in a helicopter
to evacuate the wounded. The
landscape is dense with overgrown
jungle. The troops are soaked
with sweat, and the fighting has
clearly been fierce.
One thinks of Robert Capa's
famous admonition: 'If your pictures aren't good enough, you
aren't close enough.' No problem
here. We're close enough.

20 **Arthur Greenspon**
USA
*Paratrooper signals
in medical evacuation
helicopter*
HUE, SOUTH VIETNAM
APRIL, 1968   **20**

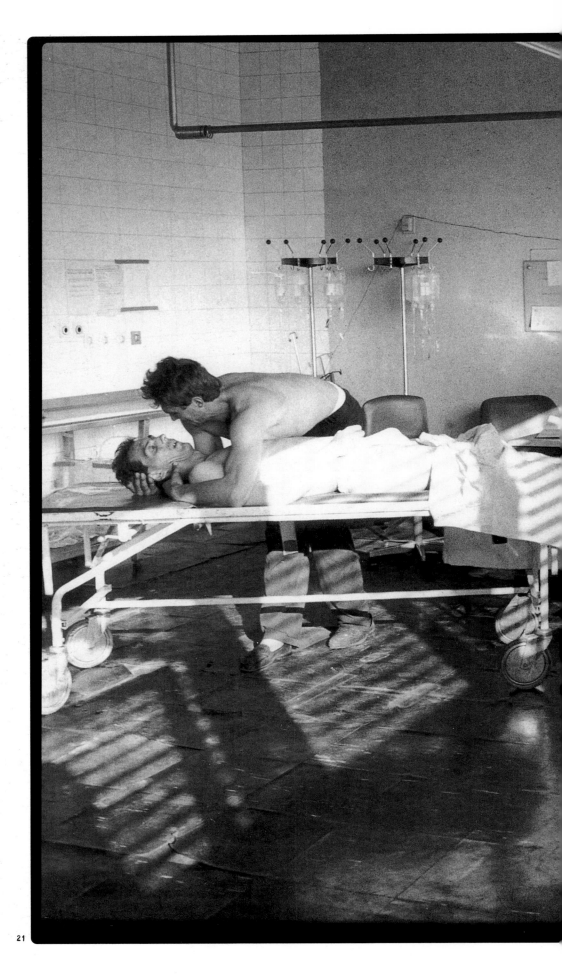

In the motionlessness of this scene, there is movement. Light streams into the room. The life of the dead brother streams out. The strength of the light suggests it is late in the day. Soon it will be dark. The nurse slumps wearily beneath a bandaged window, broken in the recent shelling. This depiction of the moment after was made by Luc Delahaye during a week he spent in an emergency ward in Sarajevo. It reminds us that not all combat photography is bloody. This image chooses, instead, to tell us that the high cost of death on the battlefield is paid not only by the dead soldier, but also by the surviving family members who will have plenty of time to live with his memory.

21

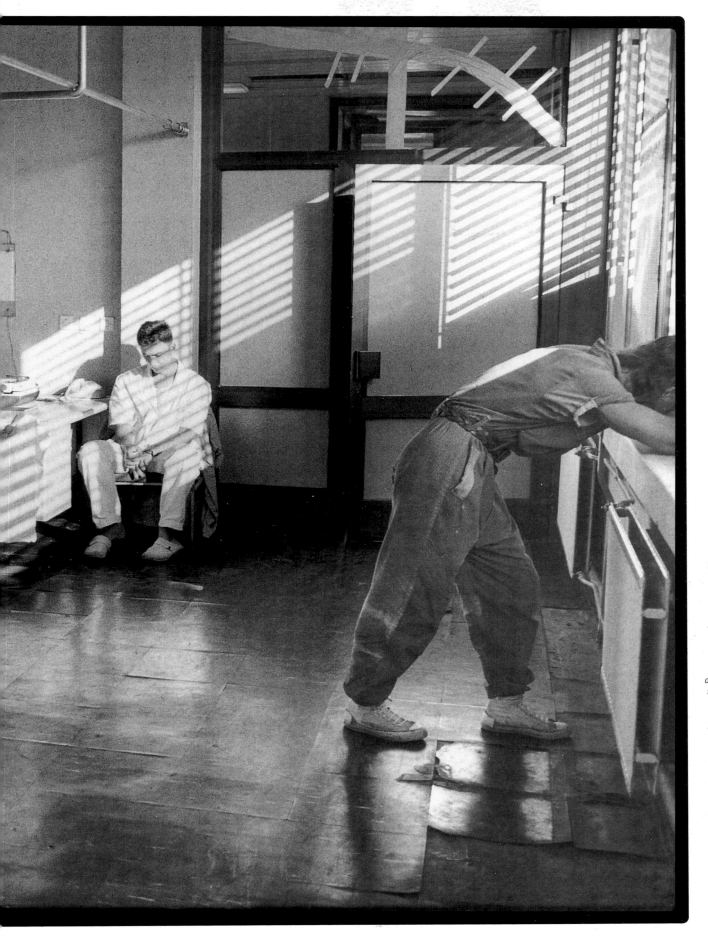

21 Luc Delahaye
FRANCE
*Bosnian soldier
Remzija Aljukic,
wounded by sniper
fire, was brought to
an emergency ward
by his two brothers.
The doctors tried to
revive him, but he
died moments before
the brothers entered
the room*
**KOSEVO HOSPITAL
SARAJEVO, JULY, 1993**

The strength of this picture is in its brushstrokes. Larry Towell has defied the laws of composition by allowing the young Salvadoran rebel's Kalashnikov to slice right through the centre of his image, effectively cutting it in half.

The framing is provocative due to the unexpected cropping of the subject's face just below his nose, giving the scene immediacy. The difference in size between the monumental half-head in the foreground and the tiny full figure in the background, lends the photograph theatricality. At the same time, the sculptural quality of the head is juxtaposed beautifully with the rocky road, due to the low angle Towell decided to take when making the picture. The tactility of the photograph is further emphasized by the upturned soles of the shoes that protrude from the barrel of the gun. It is a stunning depiction of visual daring and originality at work - a *tour de force*.

22 Larry Towell
CANADA
An FMLN guerilla in the village of
San Jose Las Flores, Chalatenango
EL SALVADOR, 1991

23

In its simplest form, the job of the photojournalist is to observe for others. Photographers show us what they think we should see.

The tangled knot of humanity on this boat made any attempt at composing this picture impossible. No matter how a photographer framed this image, there would always be stray leg or elbow disrupting the balance of the composition. Coming upon this Bosch-like mass of bodies Tanner recognized the extraordinary impact of the scene. The evidence of this picture is irrefutable. It is documentary photography at its purest. Over the past forty years, there has been a steady rise in the number of harsh photographs. Photojournalism presents readers with ever more graphic pictures of violence, suffering, and corpses. The consensus seems to be that readers should be confronted with the most severe images possible of human suffering. No image is considered too disturbing for mass consumption.

Does combat fatigue set in? Can the searing impact of atrocity photography be dulled by too many viewings? This photograph of a Cambodian mother and child in the Sakeo refugee camp in Thailand speaks eloquently of the power of a gentler photograph. The picture does not confront us with its message, but asks us to seek it out. We do not even see the child. Yet the tininess of its feet tells us all we need to know about the conditions in the camp. We identify with the vulnerability of the baby in the face of terrible odds. Speaking of his trip to this camp and the deplorable conditions there, Burnett said he was 'filled with rage that people could allow this to happen to children'. He wanted 'to do something to help focus that rage somewhere and let people in on it'. Then he saw this mother and made this picture.

24

Every photograph bears two sets of fingerprints, those of the photographer, and those of the subject. This tragic photograph of a little girl who died in the mudslide in Colombia in 1985 had a tremendous impact when it was published. The suffering in this scene is appalling. That it should be photographed and we be able to witness it so intimately is also appalling. We are made acutely aware of the reality of photojournalism, because this time the subject stares back at us.

We the viewers, who are usually witnessed unseen, this time are reminded of the one-sidedness of the relationship.

Her eyes, like blank sockets, reproach us for staring at her in the moments before her death.

25 Frank Fournier
FRANCE
Omayra Sanchez trapped in the debris caused by a mudslide following the eruption of the Nevado del Ruíz volcano
COLOMBIA, 1985

26 Sebastião Salgado
BRAZIL
*Technicians attempt
to cap oil wells sabotaged
by Iraqi soldiers during
Gulf War*
GREATER BURGAN OIL FIELD
KUWAIT, APRIL, 1991

26

The most influential documentary photographers make pictures characterized by a highly personal artistic vision, as in the painterly photojournalism of Sebastião Salgado. This photograph of American oil workers exhausted from trying to recap oil wells destroyed during the Gulf War is an accurate record of the post-war clean up. Yet Salgado is after something more spiritual here. The weary, resigned posture of the firefighters trumpets a larger truth about man's fight against the fury of Mother Nature.

In this case, it is a fury unleashed by men. As we were preparing to publish the Kuwait pictures at the New York Times Magazine, Salgado was very concerned about something. It did not involve the layout of picture selection.

His main concern was that the men pictured should receive photos of themselves. He spoke of how he told one of the men that one day he would be back in Texas sitting around the dinner table and the photograph on the wall would be the reminder of where he had been.

Artistic photojournalism makes
some people uncomfortable.
It can make an abstraction out
of reality - raising the question of
whether it is wrong to see beauty
in suffering. The image here of
Ethiopian refugees is stark, yet
beautiful. It has a presence that
is at odds with its content.
The debate about the stylization
of the hardship of others has been
a central one in recent years.
Why is poverty so photogenic?

29

Two pictures separated by twenty-one years. One of the great things about photojournalism is that it allows us all to be onlookers at the same event. Sometimes this collective experience presents us with a hero. The world watched in horror as the Russians entered Prague. And then, again, as the Chinese army crushed the student rebellion in Beijing.

The 'newsmakers' in these cases were nameless - yet recognized by all. Often the camera seeks out one person through which to tell its story. The protester does not seek the camera, but without the photographer a moment of courage and eloquence might go unnoticed.

28 **Hilmar Pabel**
WEST GERMANY
Citizens protest against the occupation of Prague by Warsaw Pact forces
CZECHOSLOVAKIA
21 AUGUST, 1968

29 **Charlie Cole**
USA
19-year old Wang Weilin confronts a column of People's Liberation Army tanks during Tiananmen Square demonstrations
BEIJING
CHINA, 4 JUNE, 1989

30

30 Alain Keler
FRANCE
Polish worker
1980

One of the interesting developments in photojournalism in the past forty years is how often the unfamous occupy center stage. The World Press Photo archives suggest that photographers are ever more drawn to telling the major dramas of our day through bit players. The foot soldier is chosen over the general. The voter is chosen over the president, the rank and file is chosen over the union boss. This mirrors a trend that is taking place in magazines and newspapers worldwide. Feature stories are much more likely to appear on page one than they were in the past.

The raw, unfiltered emotion of this Solidarity member beautifully conveys the joy felt worldwide when Lech Walesa formed the first labor union in Poland. His is a wonderful embodiment of the rise of the free worker and the fall of communism.

31 David Burnett
USA
*Parade with posters
of Ayatollah
Khomeini*
TEHRAN, IRAN, 1979

31

A picture can be threatening. When many Americans felt threatened by the Ayatollah Khomeini, David Burnett made this photograph, and told us several things. It showed us what Khomeini looked like. It told us that his followers were fervent and that his image was being used to stir up emotion.

The movement of devout Islam was being built around a charismatic leader. It is a simple, declarative photo of a demonstration. There is no ambiguity here in the rendering of the cool passion of the crowd.

It is sometimes said that photography has a weakness. Although it powerfully delivers the emotion of a scene it is incapable of delivering the context. This photograph is strong because it chips away at the context by reminding us to consider the meaning of the image. At the same moment that Burnett's picture acts on us and sways our feelings, we see how the Khomeini image is being used to act on the crowd. A repeated face can be unsettling. In this case, it implies an organized campaign to take Khomeini's message to the masses. This scene presents us with the power of the contemporary religious icon. The stern, unblinking face he presented to the world never varied.

32

33

32 Alain Noguès
FRANCE
*Soviet leaders review
a military parade on
the balcony of Lenin's
mausoleum on Red Square*
MOSCOW, 7 NOVEMBER, 1979

33 Christopher Morris
USA
*Gorbachev leaves the May
Day parade on Red Square*
MOSCOW, 1 MAY, 1989

When I started in this business, a ritual took place every season in photo agencies and newsrooms across the country. It involved poring over pictures of the Soviet leadership taken annually at Lenin's tomb on the occasions of May Day and the anniversary of the October Revolution. These were often the only public appearances by the Russian leaders and were seen as valuable opportunities to glean information. Was Brezhnev, then General Secretary, gravely ill? We studied the line-up and guessed who his successor would be. Who's closest? Who's furthest? Andropov's in! Andropov's out! Precious little information was being released from the Soviet Union at that time. We scrutinized the photos looking for clues.

Who could have known then that one day the Soviet Union would be dismantled. Glasnost makes our ritual seem quaint.

The next photo shows Gorbachev leaving Lenin's tomb after being booed during the May Day parade in 1989. As a transition photo is says it all.

It evokes the earlier line-up photos, and yet Gorbachev - perhaps the most significant 'newsmaker' of the past forty years - stands alone.

By the way, in the earlier photo, that's Gorbachev on the far right.

Annie Leibovitz recognized the fact that
a portrait session is an event in itself.
Rather than deny this fact, she seized it
and made it her strength. Every encounter
she has with a subject is fueled by both her
creativity and the sitter's. Together, they
engage in a form of theatre that is part fan-
tasy and part soul-baring. The subject gets
to strut, and at the same time is coaxed into
revealing something intimate about himself.
The Sting portrait is a perfect example of
this. What better way to photograph a
superstar than to return him to a primeval
state? The glamorous jet-setter becomes
primitive mud-man clutching himself
protectively. Access to celebrities in recent
years has been sharply curtailed and controlled due to the ever more sophisticated
understanding of the power of the photographer in image-making. The first thing a
photographer often does in conceptualizing
a portrait is try to figure out how to get
under a subject's skin - how to say something
meaningful about him. This picture is
Leibovitz's witty response to that challenge.
The portrait has all the trappings of a major
studio portrait session. It's got make-up -
the caked mud. It's got a set - the cracked
landscape. It's posed - in the foetal position.
The hope of the consumer of celebrity
photos is to become intimate with the subject, to touch a person's skin. Some celebrity
portraiture puts the star on a pedestal like
a work of art making the star into an icon.
Another kind of celebrity portraiture bridges
the gap between us and them. The brilliance
of this picture is that it does both. Sting is
perched on a huge platform - the mud bed -
in a fashion that makes him monumental
(like Rodin's sculpture The Thinker).
And at the same time, he is stripped bare.
Leibovitz is one of the inventors of the
playful portrait, and this is a particularly
fine example of her work. It does double
duty both as a portrait of Sting, and as a
comment on the act of celebrity portraiture
itself.

34 **Annie Leibovitz**
USA
*Sting in the
Mojave Desert*
CALIFORNIA, 1985

34

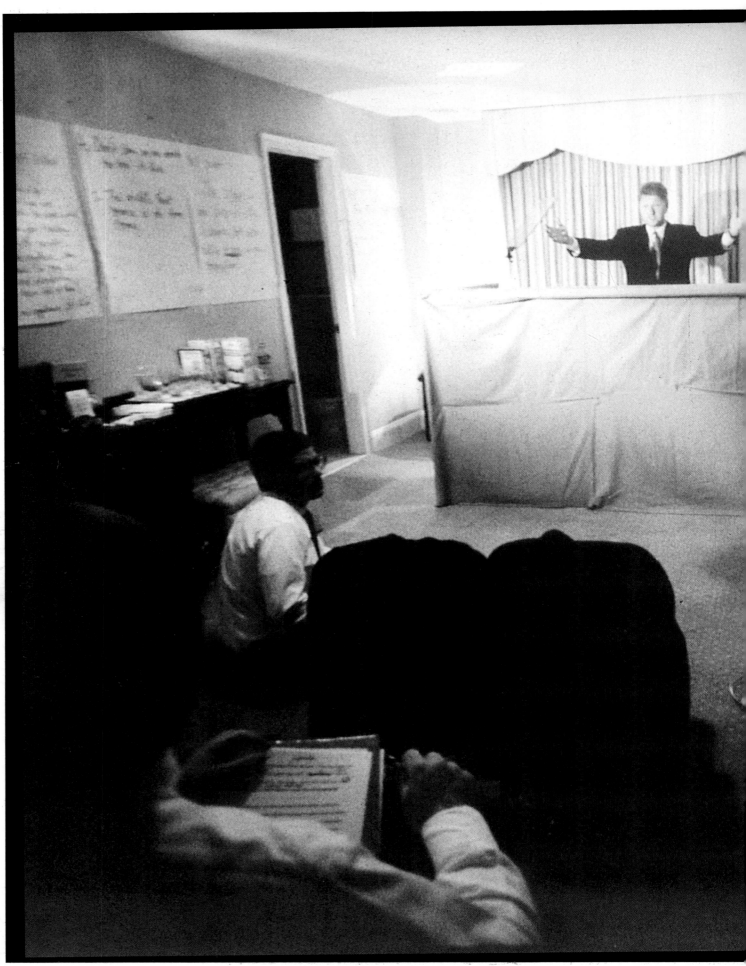

35

I am always interested in photographs of what is not supposed to be happening in front of the camera.

Anyone who has ever delivered a speech is curious as to how others do it. Here we see President Clinton preparing for a campaign speech. Who would have known that a fake stage has been built for the rehearsal? The walls covered with cue cards? The dry run filmed? This backstage photo reveals more than the actual speech.

Perhaps the most detested phrase in photojournalism today is 'photo-op'. Over the past forty years, the coverage of world leaders has grown increasingly more difficult as governments have perfected the art of the 'photo-opportunity'. Meaningful access is strictly curtailed and instead, photographers are asked to cover carefully orchestrated events. This manipulative strategy aims to prevent the public from forming well-rounded opinions of those they elect to office.

As it reveals what is usually outside the frame, this picture wryly comments on the nature of public figures. In observing the puppet-like Clinton perform for his handlers, we chuckle at the thought that for once it is the politician being manipulated, and not the audience.

35 P.F. Bentley
USA
US Democratic Party presidential candidate Clinton rehearses his nomination acceptance speech
1992

There is little new under the sun for photojournalists to cover. As history repeats itself, we seem to revisit the same places again and again. For that reason, this chapter ends with a picture of a man on the moon. It truly represents a first. Imagine for a moment this event if you hadn't seen a photograph of it.

36 **Neil A. Armstrong**
USA
Astronaut Edwin Aldrin
deploys measuring
instruments near
the lunar module
SEA OF TRANQUILITY
JULY, 1969

CHRISTIAN CAUJOLL

THE
THI

A VIS

CLIC

FROM THE WORLD PRE

ORLD PRESS PHOTO

PRESS AND

TEREOTYPES

L GRAMMAR OR SIMPLE

S?

S PHOTO ARCHIVE

Christian Caujolle

The World Press Photo,
the Press and
Stereotypes

A visual grammar or
simple clichés?

The World Press Photo awards and the catalogues which have accompanied its exhibitions since 1962 are incontestably the best possible documentary sources for anyone wishing to analyze the nature and evolution of press photography over the past forty years. Those who immerse themselves in the complete collection of catalogues will be confronted by the self-image of professional photographic editors. Indeed, the kind of aesthetic displayed here is the same which the press applies to the photography it utilizes and manipulates to produce information.

There has been a perceptible evolution over the past ten years in the choice of photographs which have been awarded the most important prizes by the various juries of World Press Photo, and this change has become more radical in the past five years. To put it simply, the question of photography, meaning the whole matter of the stylistic approach, has become a determining element whereas it was for a long time subordinate to what was generally called the journalistic importance of an image. There has been a large-scale return to black and white of very high quality while the magazine press is mainly in colour; Magnum, Contact, VU, Network, Katz and other agencies have accumulated trophies and promoted the concept of photographer as author. Recent crops from World Press Photo have returned to that preoccupation with photographic excellence which sometimes went unrewarded in previous decades. Might one conclude that the profession is suffering from a twinge of conscience and is rewarding a type of photography which it publishes rarely and badly? And might one see this as a positive sign for the future? In view of the number of talented young photographers who dream of being able to live by their work, one can only hope so.

In order to understand this salutary development it is once again necessary to go back in time. One of the most telling anecdotes is of my first participation in the jury, in 1985, when Howard Chapnick was president of our motley group, by which time I had been the photographic editor of *Libération* for four years. I greatly respected Howard Chapnick (who was the friend of W. Eugene Smith), the exemplary director of the Black Star Agency, and I was truly happy to be able to meet him and work with him for an entire week. However though we always remained on cordial terms, I was greatly disappointed; we clashed very often on the choice of photographs and our disagreements became one of the driving forces of the competition. This disagreement about what we should judge and reward propelled us into long discussions, as it still does, about the direction which our profession was taking. It became obvious that photography as such was the least of the worries of a press which made wholesale use of it for the purposes of simple effectiveness, exploiting the mendacious postulate which seeks to persuade us. 'It's true because it's in the papers and it's even more true because it's in the photographs.'

The debate naturally turned to whether one should reward what one considered to be the best photograph, whatever the subject, or whether it was necessary to highlight the most important event. This discussion proved in negative fashion that it was rare for the two to coincide.

In fact, a study of the list of prize-winners shows that none of the important events were absent. Even if they were sometimes represented, with the notable exceptions, by mediocre photographs (I am thinking of certain earthquakes). It can also be seen that many (too many) photographs of no importance were loaded with medals. It is fascinating to investigate the reasons for this.

World Press Photo both faithfully mirrors and distorts the contradictions that the press entertains in its relationship with photography. In the main it consists (increasingly) of banal illustration: photography as a supplement to what is real, but in relation both to the text and to the views of the medium. Since the decision-makers in the press are individuals whose culture is above all a text culture (or else a press culture, that is, a culture of press conventions), they are afraid of pictures which they know are terribly powerful, for they are unable to show the real truth and are vulnerable to all kinds of manipulation. Their natural instinct is that of self-protection, the repetition of well-known types of pictures, hence the consecration and protection of certain stereotypes. Among the latter, wavering between 'shock value' and 'pretty', the so-called 'symbolic' picture, which is supposed to 'summarize in a single image' the complexity of a situation, is finding favor with publications.

This explains why World Press Photo became the *de facto* defender of a series of gratuitous, even silly pictures in which children and animals feature prominently, and why anecdotes were often hyped up (sports and 'bizarre' or 'amusing' portraits of famous people rank first in this category); the juries recognized stereotypes which they thought readers liked and which became, for them in their professional life as well as during their week in Amsterdam, press images. It is this unlikely idea (indeed, it seems to me that the only 'press' images are those which the press publishes or is capable of publishing) that causes all the confusion which still enables some to say, 'it's very beautiful, too beautiful, it's not a press photograph, it's art!' Which, if you think of it, is a rather odious display of contempt for the reader.

By awarding prizes to these stereotypes, World Press Photo, by virtue of its importance, lent them legitimacy. And since competitions are by their nature distorted, with every participant wanting to win, more and more photographers sent off snaps resembling those which had won the previous year: for example, kittens playing with Alsatian dogs and children or deliberate shots of table tennis players fascinated by the ball (they are often squinting) which the lens puts on a par with their open mouth. If the prestige of the prize remained intact, clearly photographic quality had diminished to such an extent that photographers and major agencies no longer even sent in entries to compete.

Some ten years ago, through the chance intervention of certain personalities, the situation was reversed. It was as if, becoming aware that television is now the main medium of information through images, the photographic profession wished to affirm its identity and a sense of its purpose, so other types of photographs arrived and were awarded prizes. World Press Photo legitimized them, both professionally and in the eyes of the public who appreciated them, and this comes as a pleasant surprise. Without presenting stereotypes, major photographers (I am thinking of Magnum's amongst others) have given back the prize its real function as a major element in the world of information. Since stereotypes are persistent and reproduced in many forms, one must guard against the aesthetic of drama becoming a new kind of convention, to the detriment of conveying a meaning. Because photography is a very fragile tool as used by the mass media: it always loses part of its complexity and is reduced to the meaning one wishes it to have.

Optimism, and there is plenty of it, also stems from the award ceremony in 1995. Ten years ago it was unthinkable that the World Press Photo jury should reward a work, never published in the press, produced in Bulgaria by Anthony Suau for an exhibition on Rural Europe at the Centre Georges Pompidou in Paris. Ten years ago it was unthinkable that Paolo Pellegrin's work

on AIDS in Uganda, in its radical formality, could be considered by this same jury as an acceptable type of press picture. Aside from the pleasure of seeing the work of photographers I like and work with awarded prizes, I see in this a reason for a confident future. A future which will never be radiant, but which can do away with clichés and demeaning conventions.

To illustrate the confusing amount of choice across just ten years I have selected two photographs from each year. They are neither good nor bad but they denote radically different attitudes: on the one hand stereotype, and on the other something more subtle.

1962

37 Gerry Cranham
UK
Driver Joakim Bonnier avoids
colliding with a pigeon at
the 1962 Dutch Grand Prix
ZANDVOORT
THE NETHERLANDS

38 Raymond Depardon
FRANCE
Children playing near
the Berlin wall
1962

38

37

1968

39 Jo Bokma
THE NETHERLANDS
*Female Langur ape and
its cub in the Artis zoo*
AMSTERDAM, 1968

40 Eddie Adams
USA
*Police chief General
Nguyen Loan executes
a Viet Cong suspect on
a street in Saigon*
VIETNAM, 1968

39

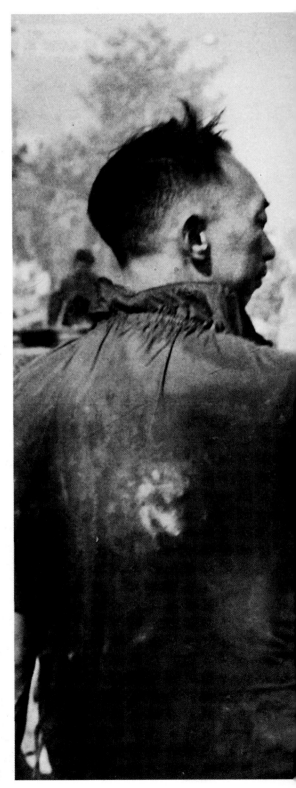

40

41

42

1972
41 Nick Ut
USA
*Nine-year old
Kim Phuc Phan Thi
runs down the road
after tearing off
her napalm-burned
clothing*
**TRANGBANG
SOUTH VIETNAM, 1972**

42 Mogens Berger
DENMARK
*Topless girl and
old lady*
COPENHAGEN, 1972

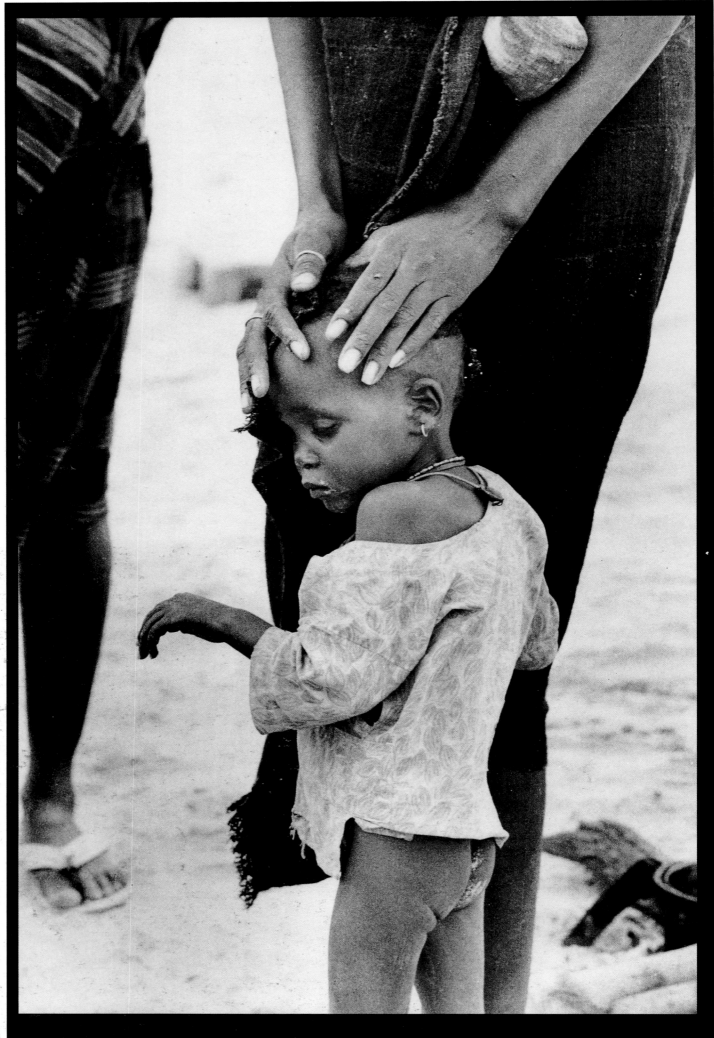

1974

43 Ovie Carter
USA
*Mother comforts
her child during
famine in Koa*
NIGER, 1974

44 Ian Bradshaw
UK
*Streaker Michael
O'Brien is led away
from a rugby match
between France
and England at
Twickenham Stadium
in London*
1974

44

1977

45 Mike Moore
UK
*Princess Anne at
the opening of the
Community Arts
Centre in Camden*
NORTH LONDON
26 APRIL, 1977

46 Vincent Mentzel
THE NETHERLANDS
*Military training
in Ulantuge*
OUTER MONGOLIA
CHINA, 1977

47

1979

47 Randy Miller
USA
Three Mile Island nuclear
power plant in
Pennsylvania, USA
site of a reactor accident
MARCH, 1979

48 David Burnett
USA
Cambodian woman
cradles her child
SAKEO REFUGEE CAMP
THAILAND, 1979

49

1983

49 Reza
FRANCE
Shadows across
AK-47 Kalashnikov
automatic rifles
AFGHANISTAN, 1983

50 Don Rypka
USA
Queen Elizabeth
and President
Ronald Reagan
at state dinner
in San Francisco
CALIFORNIA, USA, 1983

50

52

1984
51 Sebastião Salgado
BRAZIL
*Refugee camp
in Ethiopia*
1984

52 Brian Lanker
USA
*Austrian Ellen Preis, gold
medalist in fencing at the
1932 Los Angeles
Olympic Games*
1984

53

53 Anthony Suau
USA
*Woman clings to
a policeman's shield after
her son has been arrested
demonstrating against
election fraud*
SOUTH KOREA, 1987

54 David Graves
UK
*Actors shelter from
rain at the set
of a comedy show*
LONDON, 1987

54

55 Larry Towell
CANADA
Mennonite girls
CANADA, 1993

56 Richard Baker
UK
Sunbather on
promenade
GREAT YARMOUTH
UK, 1993

55

FROM THE WORLD PRESS PI

OTO ARCHIVE

STEPHEN MAYES

LESSONS OF HISTORY

HOWEVER COMMITTED TO THEIR WORK, PHOTOGRAPHERS CAN ONLY ADDRESS THE VIEWER WHO WANTS TO SEE

57

Stephen Mayes
Lessons of History

*However
committed to
their work,
photographers can
only address the
viewer who wants
to see*

The photograph has an extraordinary power to distill the essence of an event in a way that allows comparison across the globe and across time. Sometimes with horrific irony the basic components of human character reveal themselves again and again, decade after decade, showing all too often that people do not want to learn from history.

The most dynamic photojournalists go far beyond the delivery of simple information and the telling of narrative stories. This is their familiar role as the 'eyewitnesses' working on behalf of the world to provide the visual evidence of events. But on a different level the great photographers go further, consciously interpreting facts to construct more complex truths on film. Many pictures that are based on specific events introduce commentary on wider issues of human experience, exploring such non-visual subjects as passion, pain, love and justice.

It is common to hear photographers talk about 'truth' as a weapon to fight injustice and wrong-doing and as a means to educate further generations against repeating the follies of

their parents. But truth is a fickle partner that changes moment by moment and it is naïve to believe that the facts represented in a photograph will be understood in the same way by people in different places and in different times. With the turn of a magazine page, one person´s evidence becomes another person´s propaganda.

Photojournalists occupy an extraordinary space at the centre of this process. They are often in the thick of the action with no time to reflect on the wider significance of what they see, but those raw moments snatched as today´s news are strangely and uniquely preserved as tomorrow´s history. As viewers we should never forget the pressures of the moment that shaped the image we study at leisure; it is our responsibility to attempt to understand and learn from what we see.

57 **Raymond Depardon**
FRANCE
Children play near the Berlin wall
1962

58 **Tom Stoddart**
UK
Children at play
SARAJEVO, 1992

With forty years of history in its archives the World Press Photo Foundation demonstrates with graphic clarity how lessons that have been learned one day are forgotten the next. If these visual echoes reveal a failure to learn, the fault lies not with photographers, but with a world that does not want to see.

There is a big difference between information and knowledge which is the difference that separates the foolish and the wise. Understanding does not live in the image, but in the viewer. As we approach the millennium and the 'information age' the necessary question that these images pose is, 'What use is information without the will to understand it?'

58

59

60

59 Alfred Yaghobzadeh
IRAN
Children with bazookas
BEIRUT, LEBANON, 1985

60 Eddie Adams
USA
Young soldier in training
LEBANON, 1981

61 Grey Villet
USA
*Texas police chief and Vietnam
veteran Gary Price demonstrates
his gun to his son Gary Lee*
USA, 1982

62 Mary Ellen Mark
USA
"Rat" and Mike with a gun
SEATTLE, WASHINGTON, USA, 1983

Children and Guns

There is an easy icon to be exploited by photographers: put a gun in the hands of a child and an obvious irony emerges. By juxtaposing assumed innocence with obvious evil these images talk about our present and our future and questions are asked about the role of one generation educating the next. But the adult world is itself naïve by failing to question more deeply, and whether such education is good or bad would seem to depend entirely on our own ideological perspective.

61

62

63

63 Eddie Adams
USA
*Police chief General
Nguyen Loan executes
a Vietcong suspect on a
street in Saigon*
VIETNAM, 1968

64 Bojan Stojanovic
*Execution of an alleged
sniper in Brcko*
BOSNIA-HERZEGOVINA, 1992

To End A War

It has been said that Eddie Adams´ picture of the execution on a Saigon street forced nations to reconsider the purpose of the war in Vietnam. And yet the same circumstance is caught on film twenty-five years later in Bosnia, and the world shrugs its shoulders to say, 'Who cares?' The difference does not lie in the event or the photograph, but in our perception of its significance.

64

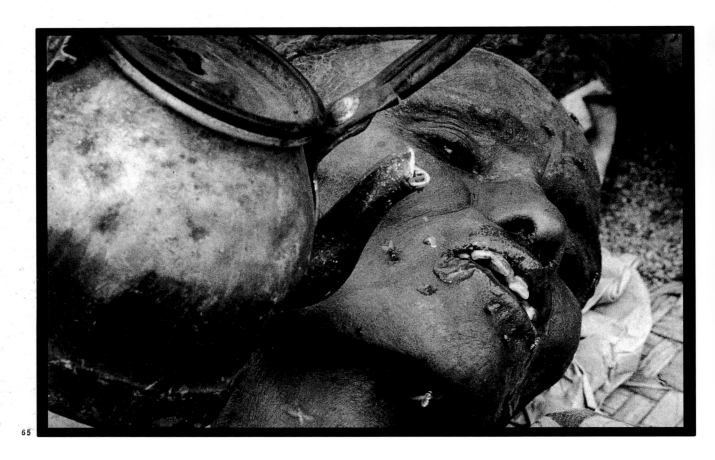

65

66

Famine

Famine in Africa first became newsworthy for the industrialized world in 1967 with the circumstances of the war in Biafra causing massive deprivation and death to innocent civilians. But now we know that it was only the first of several similar catastrophes: all the horrors of Ethiopia in 1974 and 1984, and Somalia in 1992 could have been avoided if the lessons had been learned. While the northern world develops a periodic interest in observing these events very little is done to prevent their repetition.

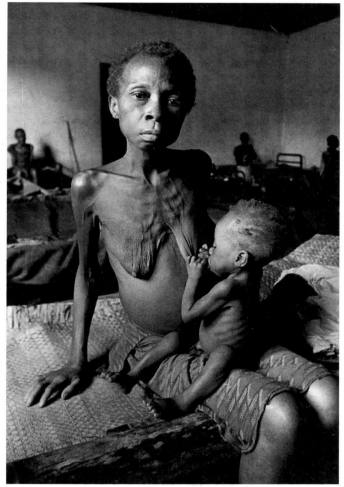

67

65 **Lars Åström**
SWEDEN
Starving woman
WOLLO PROVINCE
ETHIOPIA, 1973

66 **James Nachtwey**
USA
*Traditional washing
of the dead bodies*
SOMALIA, 1992

67 **Don McCullin**
UK
Biafran mother breastfeeding
1969

68 **Steve Bent**
UK
Mother breastfeeding
BATHI CAMP
ETHIOPIA, 1984

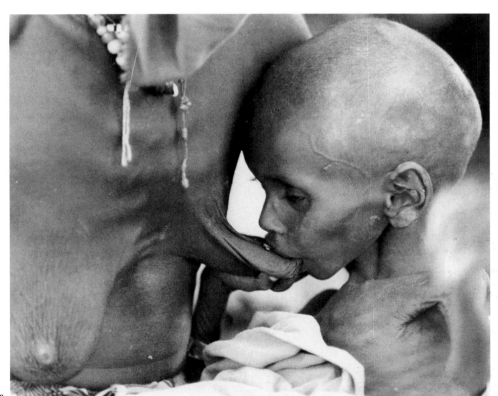

68

69

69 Terry Fincher
UK
US Marine weeping
VIETNAM, 1968

70 Rick Merron
USA
*US helicopters in the
Mekong Delta*
VIETNAM, 1967

71 Alain Ernoult
FRANCE
*US Apache helicopters
during the Gulf War*
1991

72 David C. Turnley
USA
*US Sergeant Ken Kozakiewicz
cries as he learns that
the body bag, next to him in
the medical evacuation
helicopter, contains the body
of his friend killed by
'friendly fire'*
IRAQ/KUWAIT, 1991

70

Actors on the World Stage

The events are real. The pain is real. But their existence on film is strangely unreal. A cultural distortion began in Vietnam when photographers developed a visual iconography of war that has become part of our photographic legacy.

It was repeated in the representations of the Gulf conflict of 1991, and has been mimicked in countless Hollywood movies. Comparing the pictures of the 1960s and the 1990s one is pushed to ask: 'How much does history shape photography, and how much does photography shape our perception of history?'

71

72

73 **Kyoichi Sawada**
JAPAN
*US troops drag the body
of Viet Cong soldier*
1966

74 **Paul Watson**
CANADA
*Body of a US soldier
dragged through streets
of Mogadishu*
SOMALIA, 1993

73

74

The World's Police Force

The echo that resonates between these two pictures goes beyond the merely visual repetition of an execution. These two lynchings are separated by nearly thirty years and many thousands of miles, but they are connected by a grotesque irony.

In 1965 the Americans strode confidently across foreign soil as they established themselves as 'the world´s police force', but by 1993 the limitations of their military might were only just becoming recognized, and this death in Somalia did more to force a reassessment of the American role overseas than any other single event.

75 **Eric Piper**
UK
*Guillemot covered in oil
spilled from the grounded
tanker Torrey Canyon,
off Land's End*
UK, 1967

76 **Eric Mencher**
USA
*Oil-soaked bird held by
rescue worker after the
Exxon Valdez disaster,
Prince William Sound*
ALASKA, 1989

77 **Sebastião
Salgado**
BRAZIL
*Firefighter knocked
unconscious by a blast of
gas, Greater Burhan Oil
Field*
KUWAIT, 1991

78 **Henri Bureau**
FRANCE
Burning oil fields
ABADAN, IRAN, 1980

79 **Sebastião
Salgado**
BRAZIL
*Oil-stained bird from the
Kuwait royal aviary*
1991

80 **Natalie Fobes**
USA
*Oil-covered common murre
makes a futile attempt to
fly, Prince William Sound*
ALASKA, 1989

81 **Claudio Herdener**
ARGENTINA
*Dead bird caught in a
waste oil pool*
PATAGONIA
ARGENTINA, 1993

75

78

76

77

79

The Environment - a Price Worth Paying

In 1966 the wreck of the Torrey Canyon oil tanker caused international pollution on a huge scale. The world threw up its hands
in horror and asked how could this be allowed to happen?
By 1995 the event is commonplace, and is regarded as an acceptable
risk of keeping the industrialized world working. Whether caused
by war or by accident, 'These things happen'.

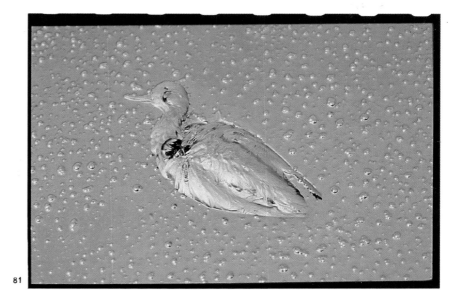

FROM THE WORLD

SHAHIDUL ALAM
PRESS PHOTO ARCHIVE
FAMILIES OF MAN

"ABOVE ALL OTHER TRUTHS
LIES
MAN, AND THERE IS NONE
ABOVE"
NAZRUL ISLAM

Shahidul Alam

Families of Man

*"Above all other truths
lies Man, and there is
none above ..."*
Nazrul Islam

It has a pleasant ring to it, the word
'family'. It smells of home-cooked food,
of worn comfortable clothes, of hugs, of
huddling up by the fire, of someone
drying up the tears. So very different from
the word 'I', smelling of arrogance and
power, giving way to the romance of 'we',
and to the warmth of the Family, but then
reverting to the strength and solidarity
of the Clan, to the righteous indignation of
the Nation. Country, religion, and race
are families that people are meant to die
for. Suddenly it is brave to kill innocent
people, noble to die needlessly, patriotic
to be deceitful, to cause immeasurable
suffering for 'their own good'.
Big brothers take on the collective burden
of protecting the weak, and decide what
is best for them, while politicians talk of
'returning to traditional values'.

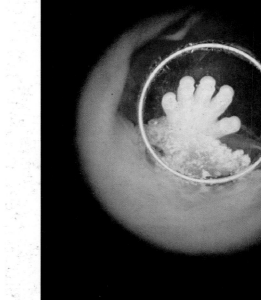

82

83

84

FAMILY

82 Alexander Tsiaras
USA
*Hand of a six-week old human
embryo photographed inside
the womb*
**MOUNT SINAI HOSPITAL
HARTFORD, CONNECTICUT
USA, 1983**

83 Eddie Adams
USA
Embrace
1982

84 Søren Lorenzen
DENMARK
*Polish farmer plays with
his granddaughter*
GUTY, POLAND, 1993

NATION

85 Larry Towell
CANADA
Israeli settlers demonstrate
against the peace accord
between Israel and the PLO
EAST JERUSALEM
ISRAEL, 1993

86 Brian Harris
UNITED KINGDOM
US Presidential candidate
Michael Dukakis on campaign
trail in California
1988

This wonderful being, so capable of great love, of magical sensitivity, of immense resolve, of awesome strength, of such wonderful tenderness, has been responsible for the greatest crimes to mankind. Virtually all wars have emerged from our refusal to accept that there may be other 'families' who have just as much right to exist. Collectives have developed which have set themselves up as the representatives of this Family, as the protectors of our 'civilization', and a disunited United Nations shamelessly serves the will of the biggest paymaster.

RESOLVE
87 **Manfred Grohe**
GERMANY
Demonstrators against nuclear arms form a 108 km long human chain
WEST GERMANY, 1983

88 **Bastienne Schmidt**
GERMANY
Rigoberta Menchú, winner of the 1992 Nobel Peace Prize
MEXICO CITY, 1992

89

90

91

Photojournalists have documented this Family with filters of their own. They have shown the horrors of war, the prejudices of racial regimes, the indignity of drugs, and have campaigned for sexual equality, but have stayed quiet when it matters most. A single charred Iraqi soldier represents the sum total of the suffering due to the most brutal physical assault of recent times.

92

93

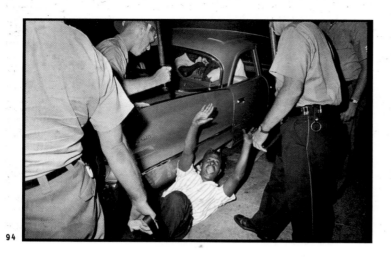

94

95

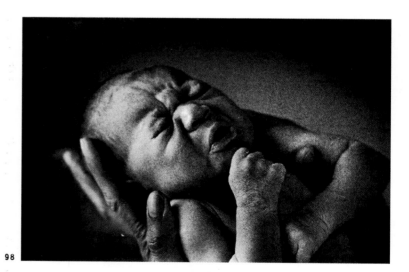

96

97

98

Was it the editors, was it the competition jury, or was it the
media itself deciding what was newsworthy and what was not?
At any rate, in 1991, while David Turnley´s weeping
American GI and other pictures of the Gulf War were splashed
across the pages, there was no space at all for the 150,000
people killed in Bangladesh´s devastating cyclone. It wasn´t
a big enough event, and the stars were at the other show.

99

FORGOTTEN FAMILY
99 Charles Hires
USA
Floods in Dhaka
BANGLADESH, 1988

100 Shahidul Alam
BANGLADESH
*Girl left homeless after a
devastating cyclone*
ANWARA, CHITTAGONG
BANGLADESH, 1991

100

Interestingly, the 1988 floods in Bangladesh, involving far
fewer deaths and far less damage, received extensive coverage
despite the mediocrity of some of the images, but then flood
prevention programs are a multi-billion-dollar business.
The flood was a better 'seller'. With the cold war over, Islam is
seen as the new threat, and the journalists are straining at
the leash. The media itself is a family, and may not be criticized,
in the forty years of the World Press Photo, nothing has been
made of horrors that have been created by the media.
No comments on the numerous killings that were performances
for the camera, or the sort of media hype that created 'plague'
in India. At a more subtle level, the carefully constructed and
controlled images of leaders of powerful nations spread messages
that journalists find unpalatable, but they are made credible
merely by their acceptance. The military the world over is taboo.
Their special status protects them from prying eyes, while mute
journalists practice self-censorship.

101

102

CONTROLLED VISION

101 Eddie Adams
USA
*British prime minister Margaret
Thatcher*
NEW YORK, 1985

102 Michel Paul Laurent
FRANCE
Horst Faas
GERMANY
*Captured biharis, collaborators with West
Pakistanis in Bangladesh, are executed by
muktis after the defeat of West Pakistan*
RAMNA, 1970

103 **Larry Towell**
CANADA
*Photographer's wife and
daughter at home in Ontario*
CANADA, 1994

104 **Katrin Freisager**
SWITZERLAND
*Richard Horse, a Native
American of the Lakota people,
at Pine Ridge Reservation*
SOUTH DAKOTA, USA, 1994

103

The early World Press Photo yearbooks had
a generous dose of cute pictures with trite
captions. The text was often sexist, sometimes
inflammatory. The gratuitous inclusion of
naked women was not infrequent.
Both technically and aesthetically, the images
today are of a different calibre. There is more
in-depth reportage, more poignant statements.

The issues are more radical, and treated more
seriously, but even though World Press Photo
has matured, some limitations remain. Stories
such as Larry Towell´s sensitive family snap-
shots over the last eleven years, and Katrin
Freisager´s feature on the native Americans
show a type of reportage that has only been
attempted in recent times within World Press
Photo despite the marvelous examples left
behind so many years ago by Roy Stryker´s team
and later by photographers like Robert Frank.
The earlier studies of ethnic societies never
strayed from the stereotypes, and the subtle
stories have always originated in the West,
whereas the South has produced only the
exotic and provided the drama.

104

105 Stephen Shames
USA
*The family car serves
as bedroom for eleven-year
old Kevin Wallace*
VENTURA, CALIFORNIA, 1985

106 Alon Reininger
ISRAEL
*Forty-two-year old Ken
Meeks, in the terminal
phase of AIDS, at home
in San Francisco*
USA, 1986

105

Perceptions have changed. Poverty is
now seen nearer to home.
AIDS and drugs have replaced distant
threats. Clinton´s cat remains a star,
but leaders of the poorer nations also now
get noticed. These are small steps,
but an evolution nonetheless that must
be nurtured if the world is to be the
family that World Press Photo represents.

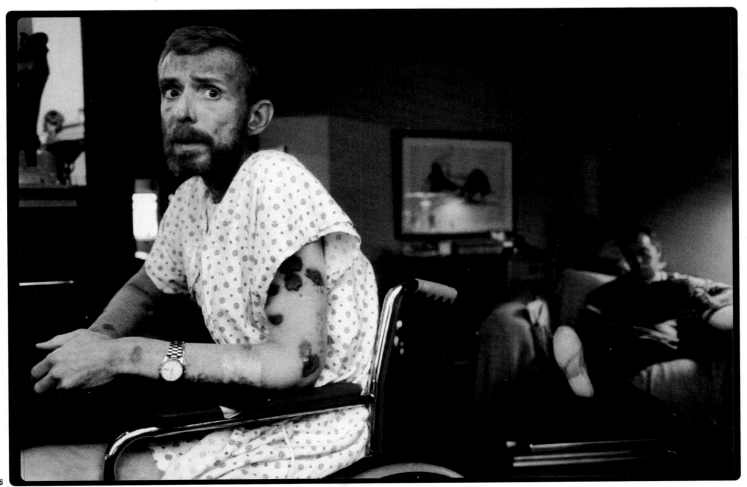

106

FEATUR

THE WORLD PRESS PHOTO ARCI

SP R

A GREAT RESOURCE OF

HUMOROUS AND BIZARRE

WORK AS WELL AS THE SIGNIFICANT N

IVE CONTAINS

E ADS

VS M OM ENTS:

The team that brought you this book: **PH OTOGRAPH ERS**

On their best behaviour: **POL ITICIANS AT W ORK**

May the force be with you: **TH E BRITISH POL ICE**

The contemplative life of: **N UNS**

There's a lot of it about: **W EATH ER**

The happiest day of their lives: **W EDD INGS**

They came two by two: **ANIM AL S**

Suffer the children: **CU TE KI DS**

107 **Werner A. Baum**
GERMANY
*The Soccer World
Championship in
West Germany*
1974

108 **Rudi Herzog**
GERMANY
*The Isle of Wight
popfestival*
1969

109 **David Kennerly**
USA

110 **Peter Solness**
AUSTRALIA
*Newly elected President
Corazon Aquino of the
Philippines making
a speech in Manila*
1986

111 **Mike Nelson**
USA
*Socks, the US president-
elect Clinton's family cat
outside Arkansas
Governor's mansion*
NOVEMBER 1992

107

THE TEAM THAT BROUGHT Y

P
GRAF

Sixty billion photographs are made every year. In order to succeed in the business, the top professionals must push themselves to the extremes of human endurance to make sure that their pictures get noticed.

108

109

U THIS BOOK:

1OTO
HERS

111

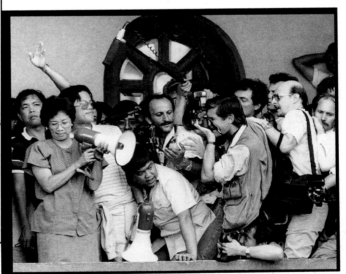

110

112

ON THEIR BEST BEHAVIOUR:

POLI-
TI

113

114

115

IAN S AT WORK

116

Politicians are sophisticated operators who manipulate the media to communicate the subtleties of personality, policy and doctrine. They never step in front of the camera without preparing their image: what are they telling us here?

117 **John Sturrock**
UK
Police charge towards
picketing miners near
Sheffield, Yorkshire
1984

118 **Ian Bradshaw**
UK
Streaker Michael O'Brien is led
away from a rugby match
between France and England
at Twickenham
Stadium in London
1974

119 **Nils Jorgensen**
UK
Policemen practicing for
a charity row on
the River Thames
1990

117

118

119

MAY THE FORCE BE WITH YOU:

120 **John Varley**
UK
Two Yorkshire policemen,
players in the Rugby League
1976

121 **Katalin Arkell**
UK
Police form a human barrier
during a demonstration
in London
1986

BRITISH POLICE

The British police famous for their
dignity and serious-minded restraint are recognized

around the world, not least because of their distinctive
helmets, which fulfil many functions. These

pictures show how their reputation was won . . .

121

120

THE CONT EMPLATIVE LIF

N U N

123

124

S

125

Nuns appear to play a very important part in society - often as vehicles of humour. No one
can explain why this should be, but nearly every year someone submits a picture to the World Press
Photo competition of a nun having fun.

122 Tom Jacobi
GERMANY
PALAIS ROYAL, PARIS, 1983

123 John Varley
UK
*St Joseph's Junior school
football coach*
BRADFORD, YORKSHIRE, 1965

124 Istvan Bajzat
GERMANY
Bavarian nuns voting
1974

125 Sidney Swart
UK
*Sister John, cricket coach of
St Joseph's school*
BRADFORD, YORKSHIRE, 1963

126 Francesco Cito
ITALY
Nun and bride
NAPLES, 1994

126

127

THERE'S

A LOT

OF IT

ABOUT

128

129

W E

130

When the rains come, they bring amusement to some, confusion to others and joy to photographers.

131

ATHER

THE HAPPIEST DAY OF THEIR LIVES:

132

133

Although it is one of the commonest rites of passage for men and women around the world, everyone's experience of the Big Day is a little bit different.

WEDDINGS

134

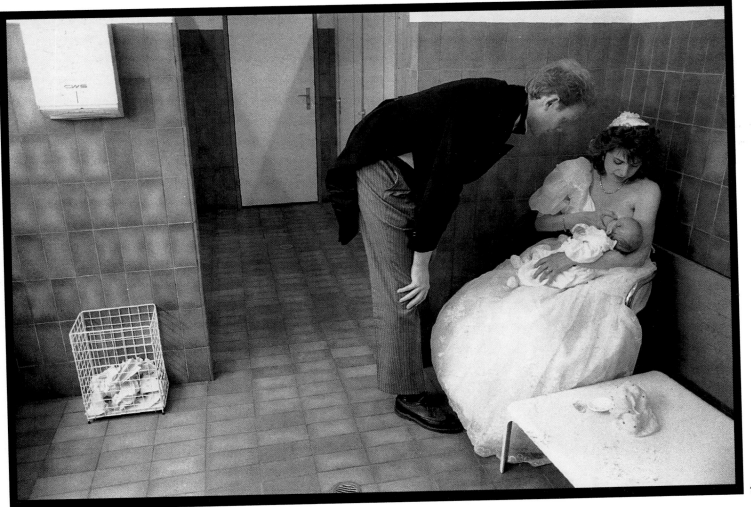

135

136

If one animal is cute, then logic suggests that two animals are twice as cute. The simplest way to arrange this is to put one on top of the other, and this tradition has spanned the decades.

137

139

138

140

THEY CAME TWO

ANIMALS

BY TWO

141

142

CU T

SUFFER

Sometimes we want children to be like adults, and we marvel at their precocious behaviour, and at other times we just want them to be children.
But for photographers there is
only one meaning: kids mean prizes.

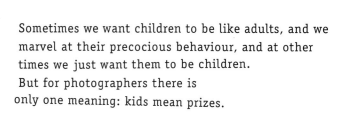

143

144

E
HE CHILDREN KIDS

Ruud F. M. Lubbers
Former Prime Minister of the Netherlands

Marcel Marceau
Director of the Compagnie de Mimodrame

I C

'*Let us look at the six images launched across the world over the decades by photographers whose timeless shots bring back such striking memories of the past. The eyes of these photographers, one might equally say reporters, have captured the essence of our solitude. The eyes of the reporter-photographer interpret the spirit of the universe; man is its hero, its victim, the fleeting witness and yet the eternal historian. These pictures speak for themselves. But let us look at the daily news we are assailed with and which is becoming more and more unbearable in its cruel banality. Man will always have need of his memory if he wants to evolve and analyse the depths of his conscience. I humbly bow for these reporters who have shaken the conscience of the world.*'

Marcel Marceau

A POLITICIAN AND AN ARTIST WHO

RESPONDING TO THE HUMA

REFLECTIONS ON SIX PHOTOGRA

THE SECOND HALF OF THE TWENTIETH CENTURY
INTO THE PHOTOGRAPHIC CULTURE OF THE AGE.

COMMUNITIES SPLIT BY RACISM; THE WORLD DIVIDED INTO TH

THE RULE OF THE GUN; THE EMERG

THESE PICTURES SYMBOLIZE SOME
COMMON THEMES ACROSS FOUR DECADES O

ONS OF
AN AGE

E PROFESSIONAL LIVES HAVE BEEN SPENT
ONDITION OFFER

IC ICONS.

AN BE CHARACTERIZED BY SOME PHENOMENA THAT ARE WOVEN

UNGRY AND THE FED; ENVIRONMENTAL CATASTROPHES;

CE OF AIDS AS A GLOBAL THREAT.

RESS PHOTOGRAPHY.

145

145 Douglas Martin
USA
*Dorothy Counts enters a
newly desegregated higschool*
**LITTLE ROCK, ARKANSAS
USA, SEPTEMBER 1957**

Ruud F.M. Lubbers:

'The courage of individuals is often decisive
for real progress and civilization.
Two generations: the man somewhat bent,
gloomy - he knows about the misery to come
- but resolute; the young girl erect, proud and
almost defiant. And then the white youths.
Imagine recognizing yourself in them now.
This picture was taken one year after the
crushing of the Hungarian revolution by
the communists, a struggle for freedom
and human rights. But a year later these
white youths did not see the connection.'

Marcel Marceau:

*'Let us take a look at that photograph which
looks so harmless, it seems to depict a camping
scene in fine weather, with sun shining for all it
is worth and with young faces radiating the joy
of living. look at that young black girl in the
foreground, trying in a dignified way to enter
a college in the United States to join the whites
who are taunting her. A pitiless moment when
people through their stupidity and ignorance, sullied
her life. Forty-eight years have passed since
this photograph was taken, but have we made any
progress since the long march of whites and
blacks towards achieving human rights? Racism's
cruel indifference is always with us.'*

Ruud F.M. Lubbers:

'Going out of your head is timeless. The year is 1963. The war and reconstruction were long past. The free world was opening up.
  Environmental problems were not yet recognized; we stood on the threshold of the flower-power revolution. Five years later the contemporaries of these girls were taking part in the student protests of 1968.'

Marcel Marceau:

'Suddenly there is the picture of the Beatles throwing young girls into the collective hysteria of starmania, which still occurs today. But the innocence of their expressions takes us back to the purity of our childhood.'

146 **Ian Brand**
UK
Beatles fans
EDINBURGH, SCOTLAND
UK, APRIL 1963

147 **Michael Wells**
UK
Starving Karamoja
boy and missionary
KARAMOJA, UGANDA
APRIL 1980

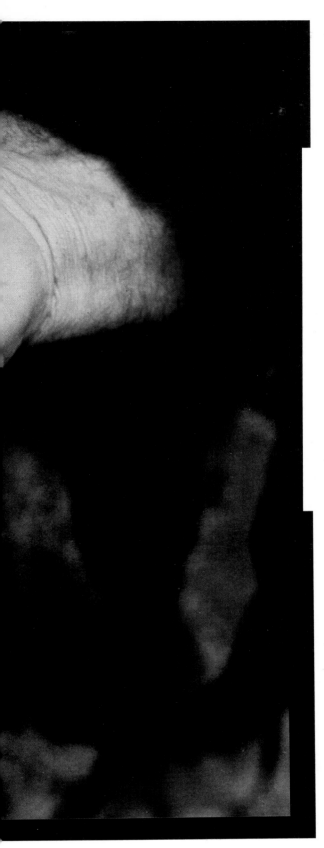

Ruud F.M. Lubbers:

'Freedom from want was one of the four freedoms which President
Roosevelt proclaimed when mobilizing his people for entry into
World War II. In 1980, more than a generation later, a look at this
photo would have appalled him. The hands symbolize caring for
each other. We celebrated the Year of the Child that year.'

Marcel Marceau:

'That terrible symbol, the dried-up hand of a black child, a small
faded hand like a leaf in the palm of a strong, living white hand,
the compassion of well meaning but impotent energy in the face of death.
These fleeting impressions, forever fixed on film, are etched in
our collective conscious.'

148 Pablo Bartholomew
INDIA
Child victim of
the Union Carbide
chemical plant accident
BHOPAL, INDIA
DECEMBER 1984

Ruud F.M. Lubbers:

'Two thousand years ago the molten lava took Pompeii by surprise and buried young and old alive. In 1984 this child was buried alive by unrestrained technology and an uncontrolled economy. Now we are beginning to recognize the value of man and nature - everywhere, regardless of race and colour. It's about time.'

Marcel Marceau:

'We recall the young victim of the Union Carbide chemicals accident in Bhopal, India, the dolls face with the dull, lacklustre stare, a rigid death mask, a lifeless structure of flesh. It accused the whole humankind."

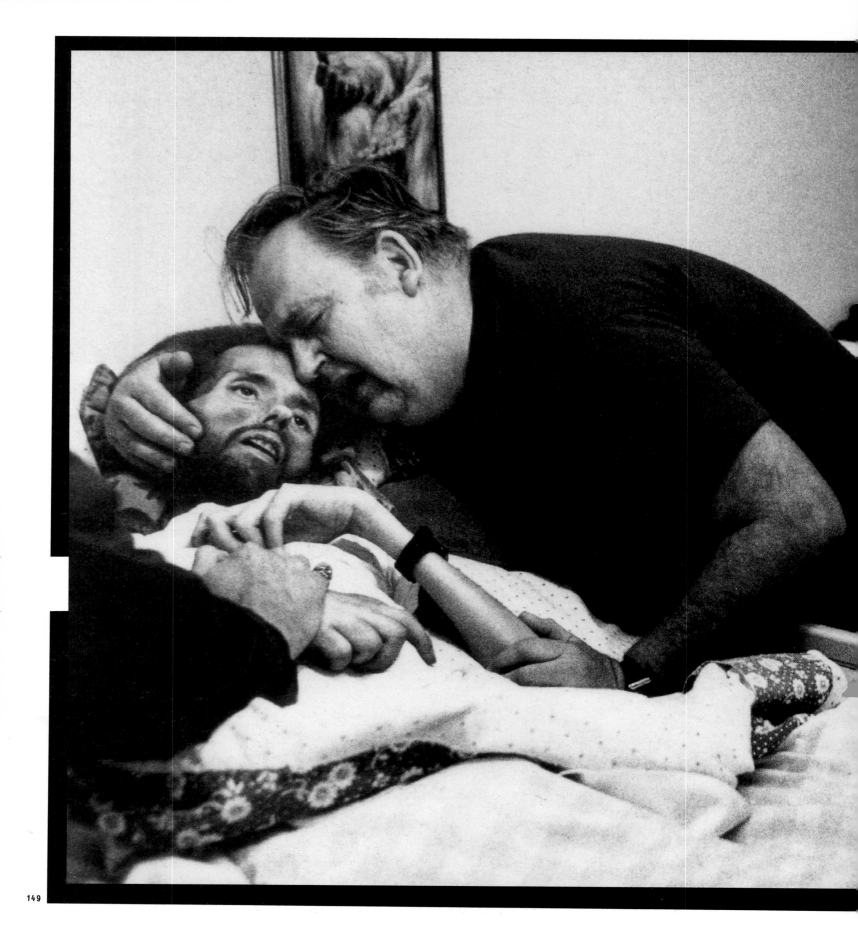

Ruud F.M. Lubbers:
'Such grief, so emotionally charged. This picture symbolizes the backlash that came after the flower-power revolution of the 1960s. The memento mori and the intense grief - why him, why this - are universal. Human suffering has taken on yet another form.'

149 Therese Frare
USA
*David Kirby succumbs
to AIDS in the company
of his family*
**COLUMBUS, OHIO, USA
MAY 1990**

Marcel Marceau:

*Look at the head of that young man who is dying of AIDS. He is the symbol of the
innocence of man's martyrdom on the threshold of eternity.*'

Ruud F.M. Lubbers:
'A Palestinian woman in the tradition
of Mahatma Gandhi. Resorting to violence
cannot be the answer. The first responsibility
of governments is to prevent violence, to contain
it, and to push it back where it occurs. Where
politicians fail, people take up arms. But does
it help?'

Marcel Marceau:
'We focus again on, a frightening
symbol of our destructive humanity: one
shows the pessimistic philosophy of
that Middle Eastern woman who, sick and
in the twilight of her years, refuses violence,
rejecting the weapon that could protect
her momentarily; despair is written
on her face, the negation of what should be
positive in life: love and peace.
This woman's face is a reflection of
the human tragedy.'

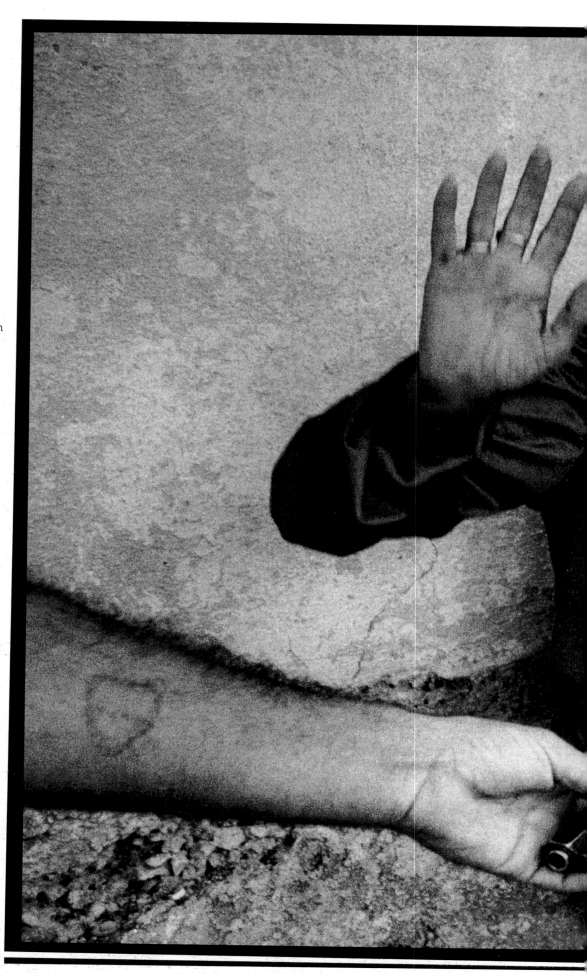

150

150 **Judah Passow**
USA
Woman refuses a gun
offered for her protection
FAHME VILLAGE
OCCUPIED WEST BANK, MAY 1992

PHOTO
HIST

EXPERTS IN PRE
FROM ALL OVER
SELECT A SPECIA
AND EXPLAIN W
NIFICANT

ORY

S PHOTOGRAPHY
THE WORLD
PHOTOGRAPH
AT MAKES IT SIG-

Colin Jacobson
editor in chief Reportage Magazine, London

"Sixty years ago, readers may have found this image droll, but with hindsight the joke has gone a bit sour. I like the simplicity of this photograph, and its unconscious, possibly subconscious, prophetic quality. An anonymous professional photographer attends a press call, a routine assignment. Possibly by accident, the result is a brilliant journalistic picture, worthy of maximum exposure in the next day's editions. It is also one of those rare news photographs which will last beyond the moment, burrowing its way into our common psyche and talking to us of the madness of war. It stands as a metaphor for Europe's heart of darkness. Looking around the world today, we can conclude that this image is a sad and eerie reminder of how little has been learned from the communal death-wish of the 1930s."

151 Anonymous
GERMANY
A gas-masked rider and horse move through a specially staged gas attack at Oranienburg near Berlin
1932

152 **Robert Doisneau**
FRANCE
*Claude Mocquerie
and James Campbell
dance in Club du
Vieux Colombier*
PARIS, 1952

Mark Sealy
*director Autograph The Association
of Black Photographers, London*

"'Be Bop en Cave' by Robert Doisneau
is a photograph that I came to in
retrospect. It was produced in 1952 -
eight years before I was born - and
was presented to me in 1991.
The photograph continuingly allows
me to project meanings on to it,
especially notions relating to style,
fear, desire, sex, chic and cool.
This is what a good photograph
gives us, the capacity to access a
myriad of different readings.
Each time I come to this photograph
I find something new to come away
with. 'Be Bop en Cave' is essentially
about the coming together of
difference in a public space. These
small events, e.g. two people from
different cultural backgrounds
dancing together, still cause problems for a vast number of people.
If I could rename this photograph
it would be 'The Dance of Diversity'."

153

153 Yang Shaoming
PEOPLE'S REPUBLIC OF CHINA
*Deng Xiaoping, former
member of the Central
Committee of the Chinese
Communist Party*
1955

Yang Shaoming
president Chinese Society of
Contemporary Photography, Beijing

"I lost no time in selecting a
portrait of Deng Xiaoping. I did
so not so much for any personal
reason, but because Deng Xiaoping
is a world famous historic figure
during the second half of the
twentieth century.
The portrait vividly presents his
image, especially his spirit, quality
and character as a Chinese leader
in promoting reforms and opening
up to the outside world.
I believe it is for this reason that
the portrait became the focus
of attention at numerous exhibitions and in numerous journals
both in China and abroad.
A press photo taken forty years
ago, the portrait is chosen for
its value in reminding viewers
of the historical changes taking
place in China, of which Deng
Xiaoping has been the principal
advocate."

154 Robert Capa
USA
*Mourners at a
cemetery in Namdinh*
INDO-CHINA, 21 MAY, 1954

154

Cornell Capa
founding director International Center of Photography
New York

"On 24 May 1954, my brother Robert Capa was killed
photographing the war in Indo-China. He was riding to
the front with two other American correspondents
and a Vietnamese driver, part of a French column that
was pushing its way into Thai Binh.
He had left his companions in the jeep with the casual
words: 'I´m going up the road, look for me when you
drive up.' A few minutes later, he was found, cruelly
mangled by a land mine. The Indo-Chinese mother with
children in the Thai Binh cemetery was a prophetic
photograph. For eighteen years and throughout five
wars, my brother had photographed the one person that
always caught and held his interest and aroused his
deepest emotions: the individual, so brave and vulnerable,
as was my brother."

Peter Magubane
photographer, Johannesburg

"Apartheid - the naked truth. These
men are humiliated by the laws of
apartheid, by being stripped naked in
large numbers for medical examination
as the authorities put it. In fact the
medical examination they go through
is a chest x-ray to check if they suffer
from tuberculosis. When they pass the
test they will then go down into
the belly of the earth to dig for gold.
The gold that has enriched South Africa,
and has made the white government
more aggressive in oppressing black
people. If they fail this test, they are
sent to work in farms, that are owned
by white farmers. Gone are those days
where black men will be stripped naked
and oppressed. After the publication
of this photo in *Drum* Magazine the mine
officials stopped this evil treatment of
mine workers. They issued them with
gowns. Bravo, bravo!"

155

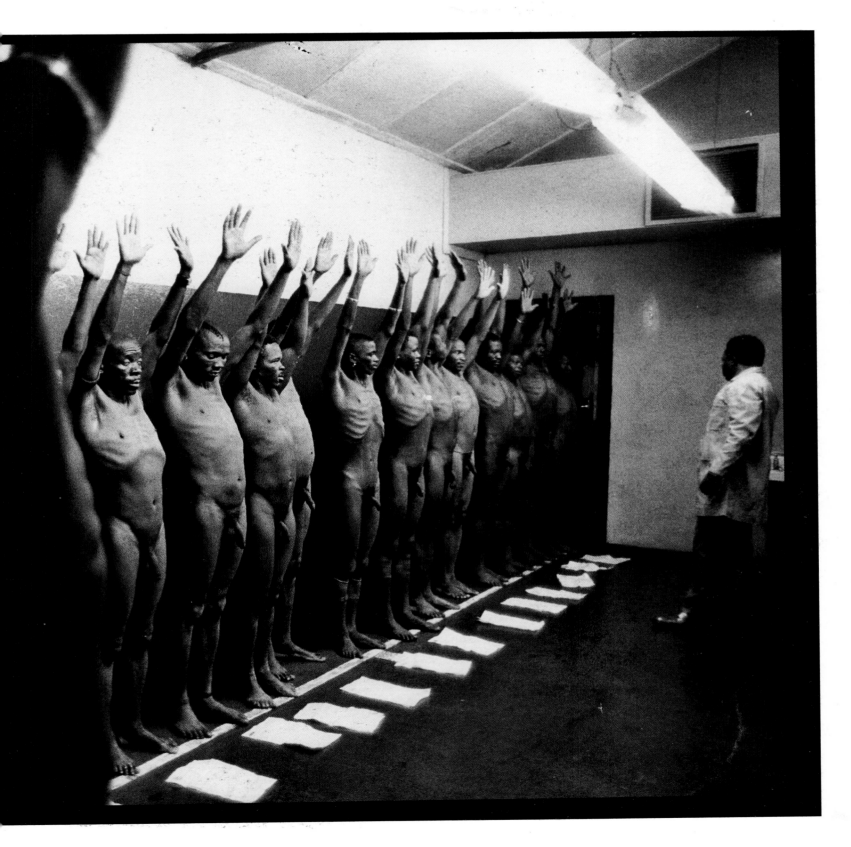

156 Charles W. Owens
UK
*England vs Italy
soccer game*
MARCH, 1962

Robert Y. Pledge
president Contact Press Images, Paris

"Wow! Incredible. Virtual reality?
Or a collage maybe? It´s like
ballet. Is it a montage? No!
It´s a photograph. But it looks
so unreal! And when was it taken?
In 1962. Taken by a newspaper
photographer. Just a fantastic
image. Magic? No, just press
photography at its very best.
A moment frozen in time. Action
suspended mid-air. What´s the
story here? Does it really matter?
This is not history. Just a soccer
game. An amazing image that
brings to my mind another one
taken twenty-three years later.
An image of tragedy this time:
England vs Italy again.
In Belgium, 29 May 1985, Heizel.
Dozens of people killed by soccer
fanatics. Owen´s image is pure
photography. No information of any
serious journalistic, sociological or
historical value.
A sports image. No crowds visible
because of the fog. But you feel
their presence. The context is
irrelevant. The image is solely what is
important here. The feelings it
stirs. The beauty it generates.
The amazement it creates.
We have become so visually cynical,
that we tend to think it is the result
of some manipulation. It quite likely
was cropped somewhat indeed the
format is unusual. But that is all."

156

157 Don McCullin
UK
Turkish woman discovers
her family members killed
during Cyprus conflict
1964

Elisabeth Biondi
picture editor Stern Magazine, Hamburg

"Vietnam, Northern Ireland, Bosnia,
Chechnya - as picture editor for Stern
I have seen the photographs of human
destruction. If the picture is more than
merely shocking, it forces me to reflect
about the suffering. Still the loss of life is
somehow anonymous, far away. Here in
this photograph by Don McCullin, taken
in 1964 in the Cyprus conflict, I am directly
confronted with death. A grief-stricken
woman has just come upon her assassi-
nated husband. Almost unbearable pain
is captured forever on film. This picture
shows the individual tragedy which death
always is and I am deeply touched by it.
The horror of war is immediate and
inescapable in this, for me unforgettable,
photograph."

Tomasz Tomaszewski
photographer, Warsaw

"There are some photographs we are particularly fond of. For me, these are pictures that capture a moment of brilliant humanitarian communication, while managing to achieve a balanced composition of information, individual aesthetic style and an element of abstract art. On top of all that, should a given picture also convey warmth and kindness, and some small grain of the truth about us all, then it is one that I´ll keep by my side for a long time, perhaps forever. There are many photographs that have found a place in my heart. Of these, more are taken by Bogdan Dziworski than by anyone else."

158 **Bogdan Dziworski**
POLAND
Old lady with camera in Lodz
POLAND, 1964

159, 160
Keiichi Akimoto
JAPAN
*Alleged Viet Cong
is executed on
market square*
SAIGON, 1965

Teizo Umezu
*producer photo exhibitions Asahi Shimbun/
former head photography division Asahi Shimbun, Tokyo*

"At 5:45 a.m. on 29 January 1965, Keiichi Akimoto, staff photographer who had been sent
to Vietnam by the Asahi Shimbun, took a photograph of an execution of a boy in the
Saigon market square. The boy was a high school student who had been caught while carrying
hand grenades and 1 kg land mines. The police, considering him as a Viet Cong warrior,
gave him the death sentence. 'Boy who is given last words by military priest'. 'Execution
by ten military police'. 'Speechless on-lookers'. 'A bloody pole after the execution.'
The story consisting of four photographs of the early morning execution was printed in an
issue of Shukan Asahi. Japanese novelist Ken Kaiko who was at the site wrote about the
scene: 'In the dim light, a trumpet moaned low two times. Sweat simmered throughout my
body and my legs were shaking.' A life which disappeared in a tiny part of history, but
which profoundly influenced Japanese photojournalists.The photograph made me feel as
if I were at the execution site."

159

160

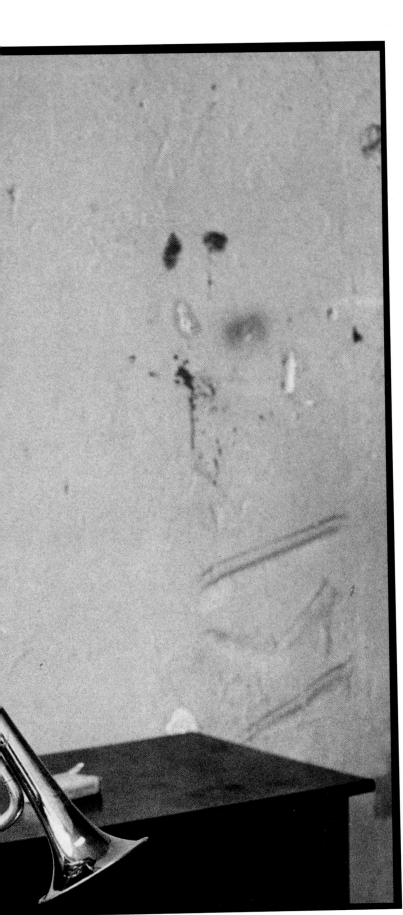

Fred Ritchin
*associate professor Department of Photography,
New York University*

"Sometimes the strongest photographs are the ones that are never published. Sometimes the editorial 'filters' do not allow certain kinds of photographs to be published. I remember one such photograph from over two decades ago. We were assembling a chapter on creativity for one of the world´s largest publishers and needed an image related to an artist´s inspirational process. I selected a photograph by Larry Fink of a jazz musician looking upwards, holding his instrument in front of him, his torso nude and muscles taut, straining for his own inspiration. An editor with more power rejected it, commenting that the musician might have been simply watching an airplane pass overhead. He replaced this image of a young black man with one of a white jazz musician playing in concert. I kept a copy of the photograph by Larry Fink on my bulletin board in my office for several months, part of a private showing for all who came to show me their photographic portfolios. I have kept it in my memory all these years, yet another frame that had been judged too ambiguous, perhaps too provocative, for the viewer."

161 Larry Fink
USA
Jazz musician Don Ayler
1966

Randy Miller
president and publisher Battle Creek Enquirer, Michigan

"It was precisely thirty years ago, and still as clear in my mind as this morning´s newspaper, that I opened my family´s weekend edition of Life Magazine. The next fiteen minutes I spent looking at Bill Eppridge´s photo essay would be one of the most influential fifteen minutes of my life.

Those photographs started me on a lifelong interest in photo-journalism. But that´s a minor point. This set of pictures had a major impact on American photojournalism. Prior to the mid-1960s, American magazines featured tremendous news photography and historic photojournalism like W. Eugene Smith´s 'Country Doctor' and 'Albert Schweitzer' stories. Eppridge´s work was one of the first to explore societal problems with the same depth and commitment. His work set a standard, though not an obvious or widely acknowledged one, that established modern photojournalism as a perspective that they could not achieve on their own.

As Eppridge puts it, the pictures themselves didn´t have an immediate impact, but they began 'a process of making people think'. Eppridge´s selection of a seemingly normal, middle-class couple was essential in demonstrating just how common drug abuse has become in the US. The work helped change a whole nation´s perspective on the issue. Bobby Kennedy, then the U.S. Attorney General, told Eppridge the work helped him understand that these were 'just ordinary people who had problems'."

162

162, 163, 164, 165
Bill Eppridge
USA
*Young drug addicts
Karen and John*
NEW YORK CITY, 1967

163

164

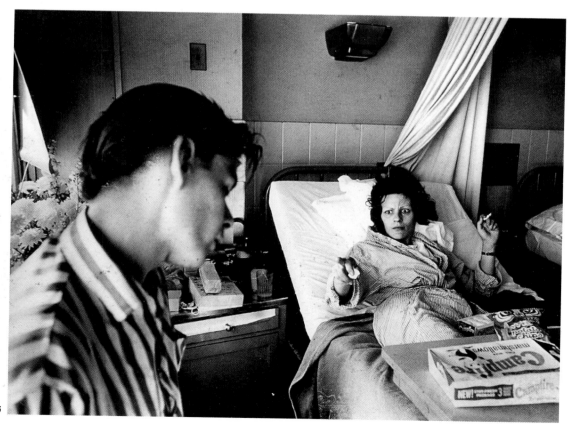

165

Grazia Neri
director Agenzia Grazia Neri, Milan

"In the Sixties, this picture moved me, because it expressed sorrow, agony, desperation and the horror of war mixed together with brotherhood which is beyond any racial difference. During the Nineties history has proved not only how useless the war in Vietnam has been, together with the tragedy of the Vietnamese people, invaded by a distant and unknown enemy, but also how false the myth of war in Vietnam was to soldiers forced to fight it. This has been strengthened by the great number of mentally disturbed people among the veterans of this war. I think this picture holds all this information in a direct way, with a magnificent use of color and structure, foretelling the verdict of history: it has been a lost war for Americans."

David C. Turnley
photographer Detroit Free Press/Black Star, Paris

"This photograph made by Larry Burrows during the war in Vietnam, is one of the most compassionate and powerful documents of war ever made.
It engages my senses on so many levels - underscoring the collective experience of the men who fought in that war, and at the same time provoking many questions.
The power of this photograph is also for me a tribute to Larry Burrows. I never knew him personally, but his legacy has been a huge inspiration. Colleagues who knew Larry speak of him as the ultimate gentleman - as courageous and sensitive as his images."

166 Larry Burrows
USA
US soldiers in Vietnam
1966

166

167 Eddie Adams
USA
*Execution of a suspected
Viet Cong in Saigon*
VIETNAM, 1 FEBRUARY, 1968

167

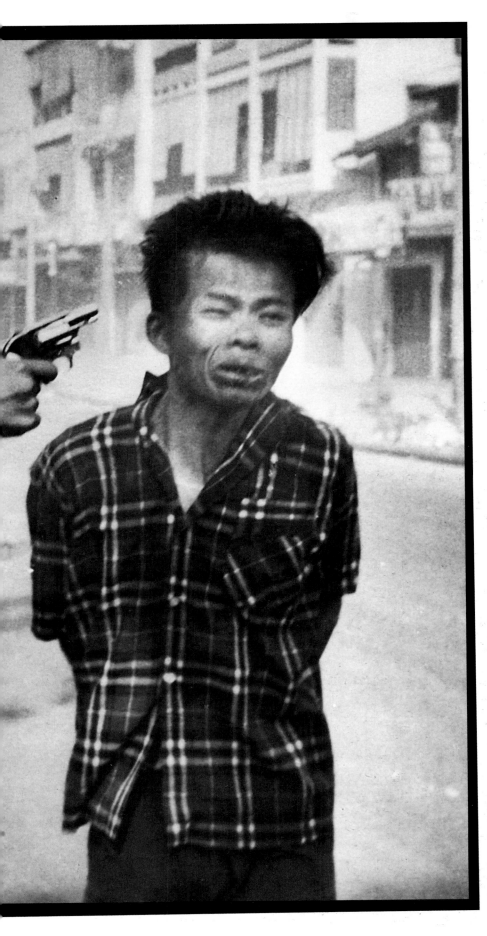

James K. Colton
director of photography Newsweek Magazine, New York

"I have chosen this photo not for its technical expertise, composition or aesthetic quality, but rather for the impact it had on society.
As the author of the image once said of the photo 'Any idiot could have taken that picture.' This was not so much a shot heard around the world as one 'seen' around the world. America was deep in the quagmire of social conscience trying to figure out what exactly it was we were doing in Vietnam. As television brought the war into the living rooms of America and photos appeared in the newspapers on breakfast tables all across the country, people began doubting the government's justification for our presence in a country half-way around the globe. This photo showed in graphic detail the injustice and madness that war breeds."

Thomas R. Kennedy
director of photography, National Geographic Magazine, Washington, D.C.

"This photo is a classic example of the decisive moment in photography. The composition, lens choice, and timing captures the literal reality of a man being shot in all the horror and finality of that moment of death. It also speaks powerfully to the dark sides of man´s impulses in the midst of war. The body language of the shooter expresses a casual disregard of the value of the man being executed as well as an utter hatred and contempt that allows him to so easily execute a defenseless prisoner in front of the media. I have seen a film clip of the entire scene recorded by a TV cameraman.
While dramatic, the sequence does not communicate with the same power the finality of that moment and the link between the two men. Seldom has an act of hatred and revenge been captured so succinctly in visual terms.
The inhumanity expressed in that act by a South Vietnamese general, ostensibly an ally, caused many an American to question the morality of our involvement in that conflict."

168 **Don McCullin**
UK
Wounded marine
HUE, VIETNAM, 1968

Luc Delahaye
photographer Magnum Photos, Paris

"A modern version of the Passion of Christ. Some higher force has just moved this soldier: these are not the usual marks of a pain that is simply human; he is offering his suffering up to Heaven, and his face seems to have been abandoned in holy ecstasy.
In war, the photographer looks for the universal dimension of the drama he is witnessing. With this picture, McCullin achieves the ultimate."

169 Don McCullin
UK
Shell-shocked marine
VIETNAM, 1968

169

Vincent Mentzel
staff photographer NRC Handelsblad, Rotterdam

"A shell-shocked soldier out of a war.

A self-portrait of an insane world. Through our eyes one is forced to look at the trace of destruction humankind creates.

One day the feeling of shock from looking at this photo will have an effect."

Paul Huf
photographer, Amsterdam

"The human story does not always
necessarily have to be about people,
it can also be for people. For the 30
January 1970 issue of Life Magazine,
Co Rentmeester photographed the
cover story on the snow monkeys of
Japan. The impression it made on me
was so deep that, twenty-five years
on, these images came first to my
mind. Was it pity?

Was it the photographic achievement?
Was it the recognition of what was
human about these splendid animals?
It was the coincidence of all these
moments. Due to a climatic change
making it colder in Japan, fewer
snow monkeys remain. You can see the
sorrow on the snow monkey's face.
In my view, a photograph cannot be
more urgent."

170 **Co Rentmeester**
THE NETHERLANDS
*Snow monkey in a
hot spring in the
Shiga Mountains*
JAPAN, NOVEMBER, 1969

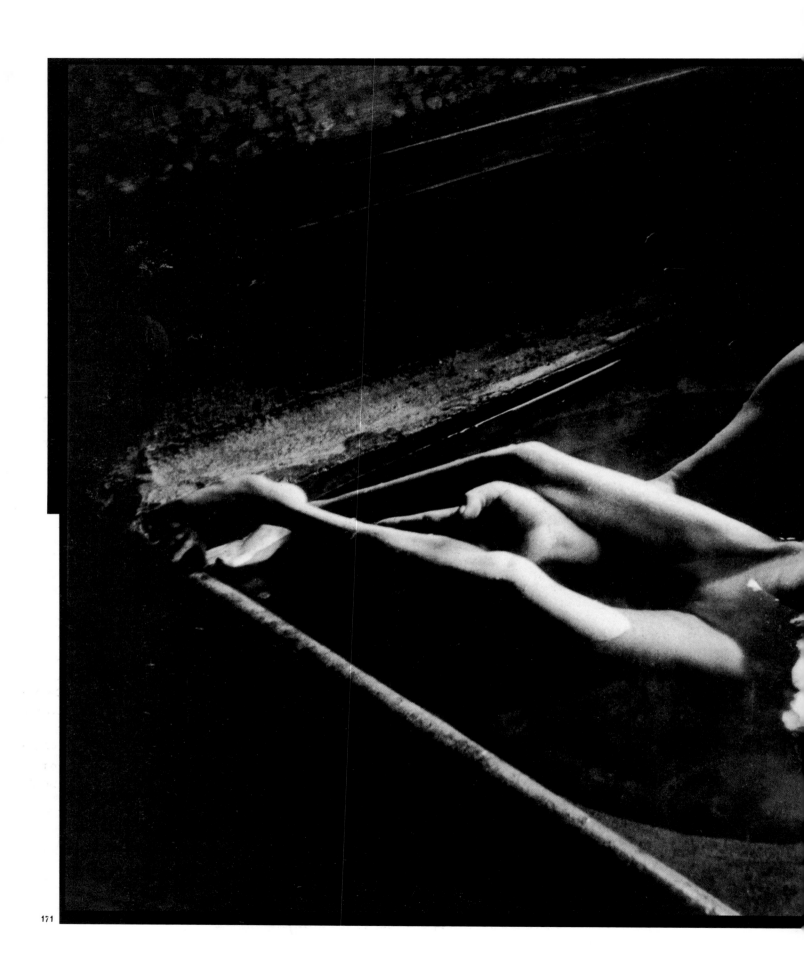

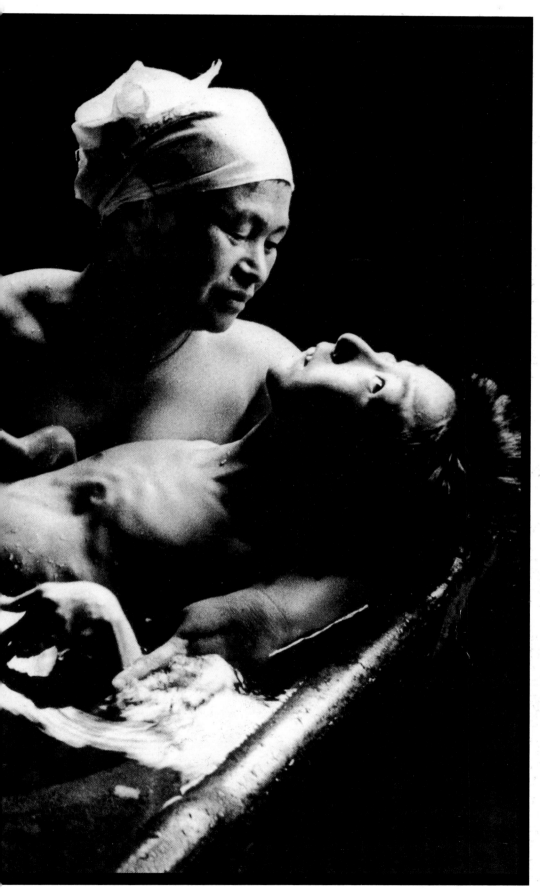

171 **W. Eugene Smith**
USA
*Fifteen-year old
Tomoko Uemura is bathed
by her mother*
MINAMATA, JAPAN, 1971

Takeyoshi Tanuma
photographer, Tokyo

"The photo portrays the joint effort of
Tomoko and her mother in coping with
their daily hardship. Tomoko was born
with handicap resulting from 'Minamata
disease', a type of poisoning caused by
industrial mercury pollution, regarded
as one of the consequences of Japan´s
rapid, yet distorted economic growth.

This photo, which became W. Eugene Smith´s
last masterpiece, is also an excellent documentary of what had happened in Minamata,
which helped the world learn about the horror
of mercury pollution and contributed to the
ultimate victory of the victims in the lawsuit."

Vincent Alabiso
executive photo editor The Associated Press, New York

"Selecting the single most significant image in the past forty years was more than a daunting challenge. For me it's not one photograph, but two which remain inseparable in my memory; Eddie Adams' Vietcong execution and Nick Ut's South Vietnamese napalm victims. Each of these clearly withstood the test of time, and, is powerful in its own right. Together, however, they define more than the conflict in Southeast Asia. From different perspectives, they illustrate the nature of all war. As a photo editor, my discipline, that which I have been taught and now try to teach others, is to be decisive in choosing the moment. For me, the work of Adams and Ut clearly stands out as a composite moment in time."

Patricia Seppälä
founder Lehtikuva Oy picture agency, Helsinki

"The task of press photography is to document and write our history. Before this photograph was published, war had become a distant idea in the minds of the western public. People had almost forgotten the horrors of World War II and had not yet awakened to the fact that there was a war going on in Vietnam. Suddenly this picture of a terrified little girl woke people up to the bloody reality of war. It was a turning point, and profoundly changed people´s way of thinking. Since then, the proportion of graphic images of violence in the press has increased, which has also been reflected in the content of the World Press Photo contest. Today, people are used to violent images and remain largely unmoved by them."

172

172 Nick Ut
USA
*Nine-year old Kim Phuc Phan
Thi runs naked down the
road after tearing off her
napalm-burned clothing*
**TRANGBANG, SOUTH VIETNAM
8 JUNE, 1972**

173 **Aldo Bonasia**
ITALY
Via Mercato in Milan
11 MARCH, 1973

173

Giovanna Calvenzi
picture editor Moda, Milan

"I remember during the Seventies all my friends had two posters
in their flats: the proud poster of Che Guevara and this photo of
Milan. It was an icon of 'youngish rebellion'. Twenty-three years
on, it now strikes me more as a vain and rather pathetic attempt
at rebellion. The author was a young concerned photographer, at
that time twenty-three years old.
We interpreted the photo as a sort of David and Goliath, David in
a crash helmet with a catapult and Goliath as the tram representing
all our worst enemies. In those years Aldo Bonasia was the poet of
the rebellion; he was equally skillful in photographing both
violence and tenderness, and in giving us a vivid and courageous
record of those difficult years."

174 Yervan Shahmirzaian
IRAN
*The family of the Shah
leaving Tehran*
IRAN
16 JANUARY, 1979

Seifollah Samadian
publisher and editor in chief
Tassvir Magazine, Tehran

"The Shah of Iran cried at
Mehrabad Airport a few minutes
ago. Farah Pahlavi, smiling as they
leave the country, does not seem
to be aware of what is happening.
Farah and the royal family are
boarding a plane to leave in a few
minutes, taking away 2,500 years
of monarchical rule. The picture
depicts an exceptional moment
in Iran's history when the imperial
army is no longer able to save
the regime - a turning point in the
history of my ancient country.
The one seen laughing is, unkno-
wingly, a subject of determinism
and the one seen weeping is a
commander of the imperial army,
apparently not pleased by what he
sees. He cannot believe that the
plane will shortly fly into the sky
ending the ancient relationship
between the army and the shah in
Iran. No media except for photography could register the history
of a country in a fraction of a
second so powerfully and meaning-
fully. In 1973 Farah sponsored a
photo contest in Iran. Her four-star
vote made me the 1st place winner. Such a success encouraged me
to get involved seriously in professional photography and placed me
in such a position that today I am
invited to select my favorite picture
of the past forty years!"

175 **Olivier Rebbot**
FRANCE
*Shah supporters
at gunpoint*
TEHRAN, IRAN, 1979

Sylvie Rebbot
picture editor Geo France, Paris

"Iran 1979. The Shah has just
left. Khomeini arrives with
the long shadow of obscuran-
tism that will shroud the
country, that still covers the
country. Who are these people? Obviously
they are on the wrong side of the
fence. They were with the losing
camp. The photographer killed
in another country, covering
another war cannot tell us what
happened. We can only guess and
assume they are dead. It is Iran,
but it could be anywhere on the
wrong side of the gun."

176 **Valeri Tchekoldin**
RUSSIA
*Television broadcast
from the Soviet Communist
Party Congress*
1981

Nikolai Ignatiev
photographer, Moscow

"Valeri Tchekoldin, born in 1946 in the city of Gorky, Russia, took up professional photography in 1974. In February 1981, Valeri was asked to do a picture
story about the well-known Russian painter Valentin Serov who often painted
in this village of Domotkanovo, 200 km north of Moscow. Valeri visited an old
villager in his log cabin who was organizing a museum dedicated to the artist´s
life and work. The old man offered him a meal. Then they started watching TV.
The 26th Communist Party Congress was the biggest political event in years and
the TV set shows the then Politburo. 'The old man was quite deaf', says the
photographer, 'and so he had attached a telephone receiver to the TV set as a
home-made amplifier. The old woman wearily sat on the edge of the bed and
started listening to the news. The picture composed itself.
I rushed to my camera-case to get the camera out and pressed
myself into the corner of the room on the floor. I only
managed to do four frames because the news broadcast was
just finishing.'The picture story ran in the Soviet 'Family
and School' magazine without this photograph.
It was published for the first time only in 1990 when
'openness' was well established, in 'Subesednik' magazine.
Valeri is a great, as yet undiscovered, photographer.
In this image he captures the absurdity of Soviet society:
the faithful old Communist who fought for his country in two
wars is abandoned and unwanted, helpless to influence the
politics he still watches so loyally."

176

177 **Sebastião Salgado**
BRAZIL
Starving child being fed at a
FAO refugee camp
ETHIOPIA, 1985

James A. Fox
editor in chief Magnum Photos, Paris

"Although I have had to edit many
thousands of images of human suffering,
I think this is the only image that actually
haunted my sleep by giving me a nightmare
that woke me suddenly at 4 a.m.
It was one of the tragic photos that
Sebastião Salgado took on famine in the
Sahel region, and was published in *Sahel
l'Homme en Détresse*. As on television,
one can suffer from 'compassion fatigue'
when editing photos - the brain tends to
go numb from visual overload.
In this case the picture had a subconscious
effect on me like a retarded knockout on
a boxer."

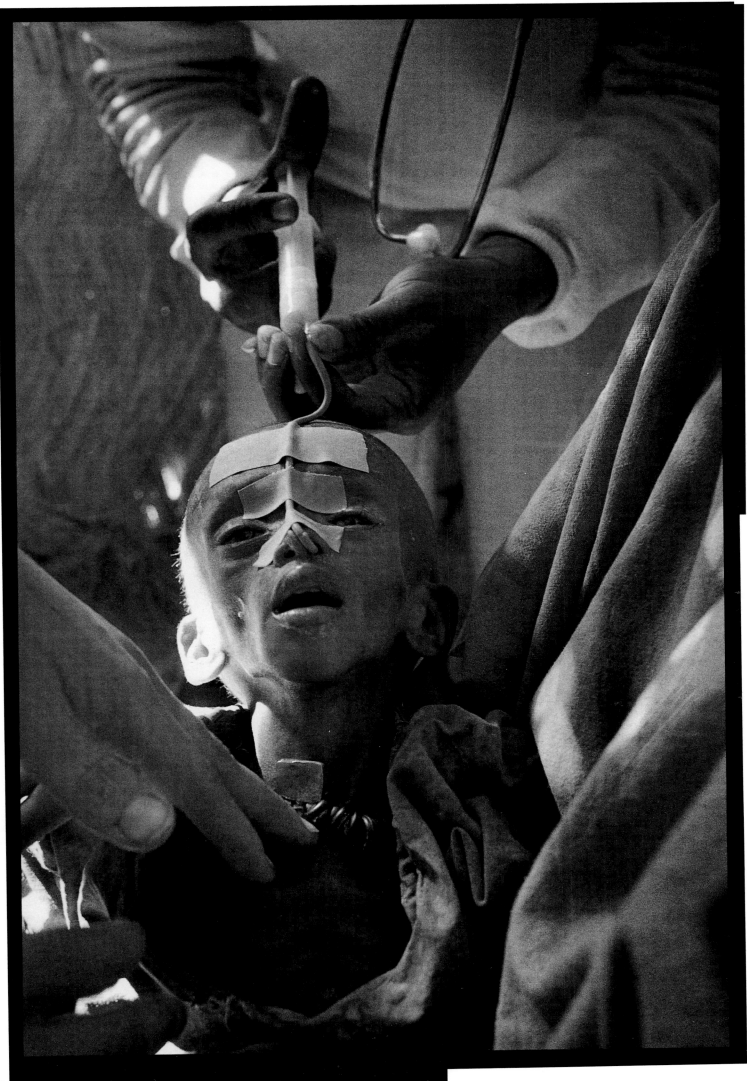

178 **Frank Fournier**
FRANCE
Omayra Sanchez
trapped in the debris
caused by a mudslide
after a volcano eruption
COLOMBIA, 1985

178

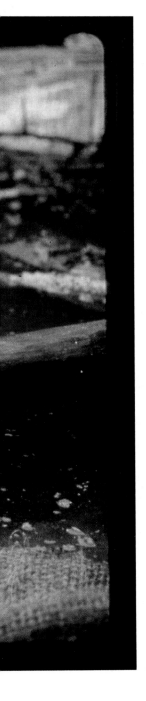

Carlos Humberto TDC
photographer, Rio de Janeiro

"I choose Frank Fournier's picture because I identify in this shot one of the most significant images representing a situation that we photojournalists have lived through during the past forty years, covering hunger, terrorism, wars, death squads and natural catastrophes around the world. The girl Omayra Sanchez struggled for hours as rescue groups tried to free her from a torrent of mud from the Nevado del Ruíz volcano. She fought, agonized and, in front of everyone, although help was received, she died."

Professor L. Fritz Gruber
honorary president German Photographic Society, Cologne

"A photograph in a photograph. A young woman, most touching by her beauty and sweetness. She was murdered. The framed likeness is held by her mourning daughter, whose face expresses all the sadness and mourning of a bereaved child. One tragedy out of innumerable ones that happen every day in our world. To the onlooker it is particularly moving, because at first sight it pleases, at the second it shocks. A symbolic icon, testifying for many unforgettable ones, honored by World Press Photo."

179 **Eric N. Luse**
USA
Young woman carries the picture of her mother in funeral procession in San Francisco
1985

Liu Heung Shing
editorial director M-Photo, Hong Kong

"1989, June 5th. The young Chinese couple hiding under the Jianguomenwai bridge as the People´s Liberation Army tank roared pass above them. The nationwide curfew had just been declared following the Tiananmen storming early on June 4th in which hundreds of civilians and students had been killed. I received a photo call alerting me that the convoy of tanks were rolling toward the eastern sector of Beijing.

I had just moved the picture of the man blocking the tank by my colleague Jeff Widener at the Associated Press. I rushed to a building and positioned myself at the rooftop, just in time to take this frame which had captured the dilemma, the conflict and the fear."

Ron Wunderink
senior vice president Public Relations KLM Royal Dutch Airlines, Amstelveen

"A photograph without visible emotions, sorrow or violence: no tears, no war. Just a collage with Stephen Hawking, after Albert Einstein possibly the most prominent scholar in physics this century as its central figure. Physically severely disabled but his brain functions with tremendous power of thought. By using the language of mathematics he tries to define eternity for us and to fix the horizons of space and time."

181 David Gamble
USA
Professor Stephen Hawking
at Gonville & Caius College
UNIVERSITY OF CAMBRIDGE
UK, 1988

Michael Rand
consultant art director, London

"Salgado´s photographs of
the gold miners of Serra
Pelada in Brazil are to me the
most compelling set of pictures in his 'Workers' series.
The one I have chosen is,
perhaps, not the most dramatic, but it is beautifully composed, almost medieval in
quality. It has the feelingof a
religious painting and it is
very rewarding to study the
detail which tells you much
about the many thousands of
garimpeiros toiling in the dirt
and slime for a pittance,
but*always with the hope that
they might find a fortune.
It is particularly rewarding for
me because the Sunday Times
Magazine was the first to
publish these photographs
and it was followed by an
avalanche of magazines wanting to run it."

182 *Sebastião Salgado*
BRAZIL
Gold mine
SERRA PELADA
BRAZIL, 1986

183 **Jaroslav Kucera**
CZECH REPUBLIC
*Václav Havel embraces
Alexander Dubček in the
Laterna Magica Theatre
in Prague*
24 NOVEMBER, 1989

Daniela Mrázková
editor in chief Fotografie Magazine, Prague

"A photographer caught the decisive
moment when Jiri Cerny, music critic,
went onstage of the Laterna Magica
Theatre in Prague, interrupted a
press conference of The Civic Forum
and announced, completely wet from
excitement, that one minute ago the
Czechoslovak Radio had reported
the fall of the Central Committee of
Czechoslovak Communist Party.
The political dissident and writer
Václav Havel embraced Alexander
Dubček, a leader of the Czechoslovak
Communist Party at the time of the
Prague Spring in 1968. It happened
on 24 November, shortly after 8.00
p.m. and it was a signal moment of
the Velvet Revolution. 'All people in
the room began to roar from relief,
they were embracing one another,
congratulating one another and
laughing. I stood on the backs of
the theater chairs somewhere in the
centre of the auditorium, roaring,
laughing, weeping and photographing
. . .', says Jaroslav Kucera 'I felt I
became a photoreporter again'.
For me personally this is the most significant
picture of the recent decades. It symbolizes
the end of the communist era in the very
heart of Europe, an era which stigmatized
the lives of several generations including
mine. The photographer caught the moment
when representatives of two different political
and social spheres shared a common joy at
the fall of a totalitarian system: former communist leader and dreamer Dubček and
a political dissident and dreamer Havel meet
in their desire to build a fair world. And the
rock music critic Cerny is the bearer of good
news. Kucera´s picture has all the signs of
a theater photograph: the scene with a dramatic black background where a spontaneous
action is directed by history itself.
A composition of three 'actors' evokes the
atmosphere of a classical drama. I think it is
a great picture."

Tamás Révész
director Herald Agency, Budapest

"This man´s face is a key to understanding Central Europe today.
The past is present: the entanglement of a worn-out factory in the
background, deep lines ploughed in the worker´s face at bottom
center. He gazes up to the small patch of sky left by the dark and
chaotic construction as if swearing. Ózd, in North-East Hungary, is
a symbol of the economic changes after communism. Iron working
started there in 1843 and 13,000 workers made a living there, in its
prime. Ózd was where reformers first began carrying out the painful
but constructive changes aimed at discontinuing uneconomical production. There are no other jobs for the 10,000 unemployed steel
workers. Imre Benkö has been photographing the life of these workers
since 1987. Old Crocodile was the nickname of the steel worker on
this 1989 photograph. Recently Benkö went back to Ózd looking for
key persons, so that he could photograph their daily life today.
The Old Crocodile was one of those he looked for, but on six occasions
he was led to the wrong person and address.
A common nickname, it seems, and that too is symptomatic.
We have lost the man himself and have kept only his hopelessness."

184

185 **James Nachtwey**
USA
*A Somali mother carries
the body of her child
to the grave*
BARDERA, SOMALIA, 1992

Hector López
director Centro de Difusion y Estudio de la Fotografia, Santiago de Chile

"This image has the simplicity and the transparency of profound human experience.
The evocative sweetness of love and the acceptance of death, but dramatized by the
plague that is famine. The sublime act of offering the child to the earth is commited
with the same humility with which its life was once received. This is the profound
cry of a society that is full of agony and desperation, but at the same time is humble
and hopeful. This photograph reflects the pain and suffering of the world, but also
the confidence of man and his destiny."

Neil Burgess
managing editor Network Photographers, London

"So much of what we all admire from World Press
Photo prize winners are the wonderful images
photographers produce under the most extreme
pressures, often in danger to their lives.
Occasionally a picture appears which is not shot
at a moment of conflict, but which nevertheless
has a resonance which reaches deep into our
understanding of a situation. This picture by
Roger Hutchings is one such example. Here, in
a lull in some of the worst bombardment and
sniping in Sarajevo, a group of women come out
into the streets to do each others hair. After
months of confinement to cellars, without electricity
and water, they emerge and immediately begin to
re-establish their self-respect and dignity.
Here in the midst of the pain, the death and the
suffering, is life. The strength to carry on, and
not just to eat, to sleep; but to celebrate themselves."

186

187 **Kevin Carter**
SOUTH AFRICA
Starving girl
SUDAN, MARCH, 1993

Dieter Steiner
bureau chief Stern Magazine, New York City

"The photograph of a vulture watching a naked child during the famine in Sudan in 1993 illustrates in the most significant way the breakdown of humanity. South African photographer Kevin Carter has shown in one single image the hopeless plight of a whole continent.

When I was based in the Congo in the early 1960s, I saw and photographed similar situations. More than thirty years later, I am again haunted by the same images of starving children."

Diego Goldberg
photographer Sygma, Buenos Aires

"Visual arts have gone through momentous changes with time. Photojournalism as a language - with its own syntax, grammar and lexicon - has remained basically the same since its inception. Risk takers, people who have broken new ground, are few:Robert Franck, Eugene Richards or Alex Webb are good examples. Larry Towell's photograph of the young Palestinians epitomizes this search for new directions. Information and lyrical content are both rooted in the challenging aesthetic construction. It is an image that opens the way for the next forty years."

189 Eugene Richards
USA
Street scene in Brooklyn
NEW YORK, 1993

189

Eugene Richards
photographer Magnum Photos
Brooklyn, New York

"I am aware that a picture of a Brooklyn grandmother cooling off in a child's wading pool has little news value, and will be judged insignificant compared to the images of war and deprivation run on the front pages. Still, after a whole lifetime of reporting on poverty, violence, and disease, I have chosen to share this photograph because I believe that in order to keep our readers concerned, not dulled by the streams of increasingly decontextualized images of suffering and death, we must also show them how grand it can be to be alive."

190 **Anthony Suau**
USA
*Refugee shelter
during artillery
shelling in Travnik*
BOSNIA, 1993

Anthony Suau
photographer, Paris

"I had not been in Bosnia for more than 24 hours before
I found myself in the middle of one of the most inhuman
situations I had ever witnessed. The Serbian military had just
released several hundred refugees to the United Nations in
the Muslim-held town of Travnik. They had been taken from
their homes in Banja Luka which the Serbians had captured
months before. Each refugee was then made to pay the Serbs
100 German marks for their release. The refugees greeted
their lost relatives and were placed in this old school house
with nearly 1,000 other refugees. There was little room for
them as they tried to find a place in the hallways to lay down
their blankets. The Serbs must have been observing the sight from
the hills above, for just as the foreign press and the UN left the
scene, they opened up with artillery on the school house below
which held the refugees.
The building took two Serbian shells and panic broke out inside
where I was standing. Several people were injured as the building
was pounded. This mother and her child were screaming in
terror and looking to me for answers. Unfortunately, I had none."

190

Mochtar Lubis
journalist, Jakarta

"The photograph of the dead women carried together with other garbage is one of the saddest commentaries on the degradation of human dignity and existence.
I find it most difficult to express my deep sadness, and my great anger every time I look at this photograph and similar photographs from other continents. I send you and all friends my best greetings and my prayers that humans should learn to be humane as quickly as possible in settling their affairs."

191

191 **James Nachtwey**
USA
Truck carries bodies
of Rwandan refugees
to mass grave
KIBUMBA, ZAIRE
JULY, 1994

Masahiro Tanaka
president Canon Europa, Amstelveen

"A week in April 1995, filled with tension, culminated in a magnificent opportunity for Ben Crenshaw at the 18th green. One confident, accurate stroke confirmed his success. Realization quickly produced this show of feelings on the green, which created further emotion amongst the crowd and forged an image onto my retina. A couple of weeks later I saw the very same image, this time on the cover of a magazine. What a delight and surprise to see that a picture can be produced identical to the image stored in my mind at Augusta National Golf Course, Georgia, USA."

192 **Kaz Takahashi**
USA
*Ben Crenshaw at a
golf tournament in
Augusta, Georgia*
USA, APRIL, 1995

Fred Heigold
*Regional business general manager
and vice president Professional and
Printing Imaging, Eastman Kodak
Company*

"Over five million people, from all over
the world, made a summer pilgrimage
to Berlin to see the brilliant Wrapped
Reichstag. It has been called an ice
mountain; a spaceship; a waterfall;
a dream castle, a ghostly monolith.
But for me, as an American who lived
and worked in Germany for years,
it was an event with more significance
than Woodstock. This image is a pic-
torial statement about the changing
face of Europe - the coming together
of East and West - a powerful monument
celebrating peace and the promise of
better days. I have seen many negative
headlines since the Fall of the Wall but
this image shows the world a positive,
progressive and united Germany.
The shear presence of the shiny, silver
Wrapped Reichstag also suggests an
interesting contradiction; an immo-
vable object, all power and strength -
but so light it could almost float high
into the Berlin sky."

193 **Wolfgang Kumm**
GERMANY
*The Berlin Reichstag project
by the artists Christo and
Jeanne-Claude*
JUNE 1995

Howard Chapnick

A veteran of international photojournalism, Howard Chapnick was for fifty years associated with Black Star photo agency, from 1964 as president of the company. Chapnick wrote a monthly column for *Popular Photography Magazine* for thirteen years. He has edited numerous photographic books and is the author of *Truth Needs No Ally: Inside Photojournalism* (University of Missouri, 1994). Founder, trustee and former president of the W. Eugene Smith Memorial Fund, he is also a member of the World Press Photo International Advisory Board. Chapnick has received several domestic and international awards, most recently the 1994 Infinity Award from the International Center of Photography 'for exceptional contributions in advancement of the photographic medium'. Since his 1991 retirement from Black Star he has pursued many photojournalism projects.

David Goldblatt

David Goldblatt was born in 1930 in Randfontein, South Africa, and pursued commercial studies at the University of Witwatersrand. Since 1963 he has devoted all of his time to photography, working on a broad variety of assignments for publications and institutions in South Africa and overseas. His personal work, spanning some forty years, consists of a series of critical explorations of South African society. Goldblatt's books include *On the Mines* and *Lifetimes: Under Apartheid* in co-authorship with Nadine Gordimer. Goldblatt has had major exhibitions in South Africa and abroad, and his work is included in the collections of the Museum of Modern Art, New York, the Victoria and Albert Museum, London and the Bibliothèque Nationale, Paris. In 1987 Goldblatt was a Hallmark Fellow at the Aspen Conference in Design, and in 1992 the Gahan Fellow in Photography at Harvard University. He was a member of the World Press Photo contest jury in 1991, and is currently executive editor of *Leadership Magazine,* Cape Town.

Kathy Ryan

Kathy Ryan, photo editor of the award-winning *The New York Times Magazine,* has been a connoisseur of photography for seventeen years. She began her career in photojournalism at Sygma photo agency, and has lectured and taught at photographic workshops around the world as well as serving on many juries for grants and awards. She is a member of the board of the W. Eugene Smith Foundation. Ryan edited the book *Feeling the Spirit: Searching the World for the People of Africa,* with photographs by Chester Higgins, Jr., has helped to edit two of the Day in the Life books (Ireland and Hollywood) and was one of a team of international editors of the book *Descubriendo Ecuador,* published in 1995.

THE EDITORS

Christian Caujolle
Born in 1953 in Sissonne, France, Caujolle studied languages, literature and social sciences at the University of Sorbonne and at l'École Normale Supérieure in Paris. From 1978 his professional work concentrated on journalism and on photography. One of the founders of the daily *Libération* in 1981, as picture editor he initiated projects for both young and established photographers marked by their personal style. Caujolle taught photography at University of Paris VIII Saint Denis and participated in workshops and seminars in France and abroad. Curator and organizer of numerous photographic exhibitions, he has also collaborated on several books. Caujolle served as a judge in various national and international competitions, including the W. Eugene Smith Awards and the World Press Photo contests of 1985, 1986 and 1991. He is a member of the World Press Photo International Advisory Board, and is currently director of *Agence Vu,* a photo agency he founded in 1986.

Stephen Mayes
Born in 1958 in Scotland, Stephen Mayes studied psychology at the University of Lancaster. He started working as photographer for the regional and national press before joining Rex Features in 1987 as production editor.
He was managing editor of Network Photographers in 1989-94 and since 1995 has been group creative director of Tony Stone Images. A frequent contributor to the *British Journal of Photography* and *Creative Camera* magazine, he also regularly appears on BBC television and radio. Mayes has been visiting lecturer to several colleges and has conducted numerous seminars and workshops in the UK and abroad.
Mayes was curator of the photographic exhibitions *Network in Eastern Europe, Creating Reality* and *Positive Lives,* which also appeared in book form in 1993. He has been on the jury of a number of photographic contests including the World Press Photo 1992 and 1993, and is a member of the World Press Photo International Advisory Board.

Shahidul Alam
Shahidul Alam was born in 1955 in Bangladesh. He received a PhD in Organic Chemistry from London University. Self-taught in photography, he started working professionally as portrait photographer in 1983. Alam returned to Bangladesh in 1984, where he founded Drik Picture Library in 1989 and Drik Gallery in 1993.
President of the Bangladesh Photographic Society from 1989 and Honourary Fellow since 1992, he is the organizer of the first press photography festival in Bangladesh in 1995.
Alam judged several photographic contests in Asia and Europe, including the World Press Photo 1994 and 1995 contests. He has conducted workshops, lectures and seminars at home and abroad, and has written many articles on photography. His photographs have been published in Europe and North America, and are exhibited at major international museums and galleries.
Alam received the Harvey Harris Trophy from the UK Arts Council in 1983 and the Mother Jones International Award for Documentary Photography in 1992. Contributor and co-author of several books, Alam is currently working on human rights issues in Bangladesh.

WORLD PRESS PHOTO FOUNDATION

The World Press Photo Foundation is an independent organization that works to increase public interest in press photography and to promote discussion of international developments and standards in the media.

Founded in 1955, the activities of the Foundation center on the annual World Press Photo Contest which seeks to honor the very best of international photojournalism and to encourage appreciation of outstanding achievements in the profession.

Recognized as the most significant international competition of its kind, the event regularly attracts annual submissions of more than 30,000 pictures by 3,000 professional photographers from around the world. Examined by a jury of nine independent experts, the winning pictures are published as a yearbook and shown as a touring exhibition that visits over 60 venues in more than 30 countries every year. World Press Photo works with a dynamic team of photographers and editors at the forefront of the profession, offering training to photographers and stimulating debate on the ethical and practical aspects of press photography. The seminars and the annual masterclass are complemented by a growing number of printed and electronic publications. Operating from Amsterdam, the Netherlands, the World Press Photo governing board includes members with wide-ranging interest in press photography, and works in consultation with an International Advisory Board comprising a range of experts and professionals from the world of press photography.

The foundation is under the patronage of HRH Prince Bernhard of the Netherlands.

World Press Photo is a non profit organization whose activities are funded by proceeds from the annual exhibition, royalties from the yearbook and sponsorship by Canon, Eastman Kodak Company and KLM Royal Dutch Airlines.

WORLD

Contributors

Vincent Alabiso NEW YORK
executive photo editor The Associated Press

Elisabeth Biondi HAMBURG
picture editor Stern Magazine

Neil Burgess LONDON
managing editor Network Photographers

Giovanna Calvenzi MILAN
picture editor Moda Magazine

Cornell Capa NEW YORK
*founding director International Center
of Photography*

James K. Colton NEW YORK
director of photography Newsweek Magazine

Luc Delahaye PARIS
photographer Magnum Photos

James A. Fox PARIS
editor in chief Magnum Photos

Diego Goldberg BUENOS AIRES
photographer Sygma

L. Fritz Gruber COLOGNE
*honorary president Photographic Society of
Germany*

Fred Heigold LONDON
*vice president and general regional
business manager Professional and Printing
Imaging, Eastman Kodak Company*

Paul Huf AMSTERDAM
photographer

Carlos Humberto TDC RIO DE JANEIRO
photographer Contexto

Nikolai Ignatiev MOSCOW
photographer

Colin Jacobson LONDON
editor in chief Reportage Magazine

Thomas R. Kennedy WASHINGTON D.C.
*director of photography National
Geographic Magazine*

Liu Heung Shing HONG KONG
editorial director M-Photo

Hector López SANTIAGO DE CHILE
*director Centro de Difusion y Estudio de la
Fotografia*

Mochtar Lubis JAKARTA
journalist

Peter Magubane JOHANNESBURG
photographer Time Magazine

Vincent Mentzel ROTTERDAM
staff photographer NRC Handelsblad

Randy Miller BATTLE CREEK MICHIGAN
*president and publisher
Battle Creek Enquirer*

Daniela Mrázková PRAGUE
editor in chief Fotografie Magazine

Grazia Neri MILAN
director Agenzia Grazia Neri

Robert Y. Pledge PARIS
president Contact Press Images

Michael Rand LONDON
consultant art director

Sylvie Rebbot PARIS
picture editor Geo Magazine

Tamás Révész BUDAPEST
director Herald Agency

Eugene Richards NEW YORK
photographer Magnum Photos

Fred Ritchin NEW YORK
*New York University associate
professor, Dept. of Photography*

Seifollah Samadian TEHRAN
publisher Tassvir Magazine

Mark Sealy LONDON
*director Autograph The Association of
Black Photographers*

Patricia Seppälä HELSINKI
founder Lehtikuva Oy picture agency

Dieter Steiner NEW YORK
bureau chief Stern Magazine

Anthony Suau PARIS
photographer

Masahiro Tanaka AMSTELVEEN
president Canon Europa

Takeyoshi Tanuma TOKYO
photographer

Tomasz Tomaszewski WARSAW
photographer

David C. Turnley PARIS
photographer Detroit Free Press/Black Star

Teizo Umezu TOKYO
producer cultural projects Asahi Shimbun

Ron Wunderink AMSTELVEEN
*senior vice president PR KLM Royal Dutch
Airlines*

Yang Shaoming BEIJING
*photographer/president Chinese Society of
Contemporary Photography*

CONTRIBU –

World Press Photo is grateful for all
photographers, publications, photo
agencies, libraries and other
organizations who have provided valuable information and by whose courtesy
the picture material for this book has
been compiled.
Every attempt has been made to trace
and properly acknowledge the copyright
holder of each photograph reproduced in
this book. However, should inaccuracies
or omissions have occurred,
World Press Photo would kindly like to
call on the parties in question to contact
the foundation office for rectification.

TORS

**Contributing organizations
(Photo reference)** ABC Press AMSTERDAM

Agence France Presse LOS ANGELES

Agence France Presse PARIS
111, CHRONOLOGY 1971

Amazonas Images PARIS
7, 26, 27, 51, 77, 177, 182

APN MOSCOW

Artis Zoo AMSTERDAM
39

Asahi Shimbun TOKYO
159, 160

The Associated Press AMSTERDAM
113

The Associated Press LONDON
125

The Associated Press NEW YORK
19, 20, 40, 41, 63, 70, 94, 96, 136, 145, 167, 172, 180,
CHRONOLOGY 1957, -1964, -1965, -1972, -1982,
COVER 5

The Associated Press PARIS
102

Bapla LONDON

Bettmann New York
50, 132, CHRONOLOGY 1966, -1975

**Bildarchiv Preussischer
Kulturbesitz** BERLIN
28, CHRONOLOGY 1968

Bilderberg HAMBURG

Black Star Publishing NEW YORK
5, 33, 72, 93, 171

Bongarts Sportfoto HAMBURG
COVER 8

Robert Capa Estate NEW YORK
154

The Chicago Tribune CHICAGO
8, 43

Contact Press Images NEW YORK
24, 25, 31, 47, 48, 91, 106,
CHRONOLOGY 1979, -1985, -1991

Contact Press Images PARIS
175

Cosmos PARIS
30

Daily Mail LONDON
138

Daily Mirror LONDON
45, 129, 142

The Dallas Times Herald DALLAS
CHRONOLOGY 1963

Dalmas PARIS

Detroit Free Press DETROIT
5, 72, 93

Deutsche Presse Agentur BERLIN

Deutsche Presse Agentur FRANKFURT
107, 124, 193

**The Domestic Abuse
Awareness Project** NEW YORK
2

Dobry Vecernik PRAGUE
128

Drik Picture Library DHAKA
100

Ekstra Bladet COPENHAGEN
42

The Evening Chelyabinsk CHELYABINSK

Focus Photo und Presseagent HAMBURG
CHRONOLOGY 1967

Gamma Presse Images PARIS
148, CHRONOLOGY 1984

Gamma Liaison NEW YORK

George Eastman House ROCHESTER
3, 4

Hollandse Hoogte AMSTERDAM
14

The Houston Chronicle HOUSTON

Hulton Deutsch Collection LONDON
69, 151

The Independent LONDON
86

India Foto News Features NEW DELHI
127

Impact Photos LONDON
71

The Irish Times DUBLIN
141

Islamic Republic News Agency TEHRAN
174

Katz Pictures LONDON
56, 58

Larry Burrows Collection NEW YORK
166

The Library of Congress WASHINGTON, D.C.
1

Life Magazine NEW YORK
18, 82, 170, CHRONOLOGY 1958

Magnum Photos LONDON
6

Magnum Photos NEW YORK
4, 12, 13, 22, 55, 66, 85, 103, 188, 189, 191,
CHRONOLOGY 1993, -1994, COVER 2, -4

Magnum Photos PARIS
21, 38, 57, CHRONOLOGY 1992

The Mail on Sunday LONDON
68

Mainichi Shimbun TOKYO
CHRONOLOGY 1960

Mark Meyer Estate CLAYTON DE

Mary Ellen Mark Library NEW YORK
9, 10, 62

Matrix International NEW YORK
105

MCA TV International UNIVERSAL CITY
17

The Melbourne Sun MELBOURNE

Mirror Syndication International LONDON
44, 75, 90, 118, CHRONOLOGY 1974

Morgenavisen Jyllands-Posten VIBY
84

NASA Media Services WASHINGTON, D.C.
36, CHRONOLOGY 1969

National Geographic Magazine
WASHINGTON, D.C.
COVER 6

National Union of Journalists LONDON

Network Photographers LONDON
89, 117, 150 186

Newsweek Magazine NEW YORK
29

NRC Handelsblad ROTTERDAM
46, 97

The New York Times NEW YORK
CHRONOLOGY 1973

The New York Times Magazine NEW YORK

The People LONDON
54, 131

The Philadelphia Inquirer PHILADELPHIA
76, 95, COVER 3

Politikens Press Foto COPENHAGEN
42

Rapho Agence Photographique PARIS
152

Rex Features LONDON
119

Saba Press Photos NEW YORK
92

San Francisco Chronicle SAN FRANCISCO
179

The Scotsman Newspaper EDINBURGH
146

Signum PRAGUE
183

Sipa Press NEW YORK

Sipa Press PARIS
59, CHRONOLOGY 1976, -1988

Sports Illustrated NEW YORK

Sunday Express LONDON

The Sunday Times LONDON
130

Sygma PARIS
32, 49, 78 187

Sygma NEW YORK
99

Thames Television LONDON
17

Thompson Regional Newspapers LONDON

Time Magazine NEW YORK
35, 60, 181

Toronto Star TORONTO
74, 112

Transworld Features Holland HAARLEM

U.S. News & World Report WASHINGTON D.C.
CHRONOLOGY 1978

Världsbilden MALMÖ
65

The West Australian PERTH
23

Wildlight Photos SYDNEY
110

Wostok Press PARIS
184

Z Management ZÜRICH
104

Editor
Stephen Mayes

Concept
Anthon Beeke

Design
Studio Anthon Beeke
in collaboration with Visser/Poortman
Design Amsterdam
Doc Visser, Huber Jaspers

Picture coordinators
Floris van Bergem,
Martin Harlaar, Jan-Pieter Koster

Copy editor
Rictor Norton

Production assistant
Thomas Slätis

Project managed by
Kari Lundelin

PRODUCTION TEAM

Special thanks to
Marloes Krijnen
Randy Miller
Robert Y. Pledge
Morgan Ryan
Michele Stephenson

Lithography/Printing/Binding
Snoeck-Ducaju & Zoon
Ghent
Belgium

Paper
KNP/Leykam
Maastricht
Proost en Brandt, Diemen

Technical coordinator
Rob van Zweden
Sdu Publishers
Koninginnegracht
The Hague
Holland

With appreciation for
Joop Swart (1925-1994),
whose enthusiasm
for press photography
inspired this book.

Copyright © 1995
Stichting World Press Photo Holland
Amsterdam.
Sdu Publishers, Koninginnegracht
The Hague

Copyright for the photography by the
photographers

First published in the United Kingdom
in 1996 by Thames and Hudson Ltd.
30 Bloomsbury Street,
London WC1B 3QP

British Library Cataloguing-in-
Publication Data
A catalogue record for this book is
available from the British Library

First published in the United States of
America in 1996
by Thames and Hudson, Inc.
500 Fifth Avenue, New York, NY 10110

Library of Congress Catalog Card
Number 95-60603

ISBN 0-500-27848-2
Printed in Belgium

This book has been published under
the auspices of the Stichting World
Press Photo Holland, Amsterdam,
the Netherlands.

Office World Press Photo
Jacob Obrechtstraat 26
1071 KM Amsterdam, The Netherlands.
Telephone +31 (20) 6766 096
Fax +31 (20) 6764 471
E-mail office@worldpressphoto.nl
Managing director: Marloes Krijnen

1955 Mogens von Haven DENMARK
Motorcycle race

1956 Helmut Pirath GERMANY
*A German soldier is reunited with his daughter after spending
eleven years as a World War II prisoner in the Soviet Union*

1957 Douglas Martin USA
*Dorothy Counts, one of the first black students
to enter a desegregated high school in Little Rock, Arkansas*

1958 Don Cravens USA
Elvis Presley undergoes army physical at Fort Chaffe, Arkansas

1959 Burt Glinn USA
*Nikita Khrushchev, first Soviet leader to visit the USA,
at the Lincoln Memorial in Washington, D.C.*

1960 Yasushi Nagao JAPAN
*Right-wing student Yamaguchi assassinates Japanese Socialist
party chairman Asanuma during speech in Tokyo*

1961 Peter Leibing GERMANY
East German border guard defects into the French sector of Berlin

1962 Héctor Rondón Lovera VENEZUELA
*Priest with soldier mortally wounded by a sniper during
military rebellion at Puerto Caballo naval base in Venezuela*

1963 Bob Jackson USA
*Jack Ruby shoots Lee Harvey Oswald,
accused assassin of J. F. Kennedy, outside Dallas city jail*

1964 Felice Quinto USA
*Demonstrator and police during
a black civil rights protest in Philadelphia*

1965 John Rooney USA
*Cassius Clay after knocking out challenger for World Heavyweight
title Sonny Liston in sixty seconds in Lewiston, Maine*

1966 Kyoichi Sawada JAPAN
US troops drag the body of Viet Cong soldier

1967 Michael Ruetz GERMANY
New military regime in Greece

1968 Hilmar Pabel GERMANY
*Citizens of Prague protest against the
occupation by Warsaw Pact forces*

1969 Neil Armstrong USA
*Astronaut Edwin Aldrin by the US flag at
the Sea of Tranquility on the Moon*

1970 David Gerrard UK
*Boy holding a molotov cocktail
in Londonderry, Northern Ireland*

1971 Michel Paul Laurent FRANCE
Horst Faas GERMANY
West Pakistani collaborators are executed in Bangladesh

1972 Nick Ut USA
*Vietnamese children burned by napalm
run down the road in Trangbang, northwest of Saigon*

1973 Anonymous
*Chilean President Salvador Allende
shortly before being killed during military coup*

1974 Ian Bradshaw UK
*Streaker Michael O'Brien during a rugby match
between France and England at Twickenham Stadium*

1975 Thai Khac Chuong USA
*Overloaded evacuation helicopter
during withdrawal from Nha Trang,
South Vietnam*

1976 Françoise DeMulder FRANCE
*Lebanese woman in a village outside Beirut during conflict
between Christian and Muslim forces*

1977 Leslie Hammond SOUTH AFRICA
*Police tear gas breaks up a group of
squatters protesting against demolition of their homes in a
shanty town near Cape Town*

1978 Darryl Heikes USA
*Israeli Prime Minister Begin and Egyptian
President Sadat sign a Middle East peace
treaty at Camp David talks hosted by US
President Carter*

1979 David Burnett USA
*Parade with posters of Ayatollah
Khomeini, Tehran, Iran*

1980 Michael Wells UK
*Starving Karamoja boy and missionary
in Uganda*

1981 Manuel Barriopedro SPAIN
*Lt Col Antonio Tejero Molina holds
Spanish parliament hostage for eighteen
hours during attempted military coup*

1982 Martin Cleaver UK
*British warship Antelope hit by Argentine
warplanes during the Falklands War*

1983 Mustafa Bozdemir TURKEY
*Turkish woman finds her children
who were buried alive by an earthquake*

1984 Pablo Bartholomew INDIA
*Victim of Union Carbide
chemical plant leak in Bhopal, India*

1985 Frank Fournier FRANCE
*Twelve-year old Omayra Sanchez
caught in the debris of a mud slide after
a volcano eruption in Colombia*

1986 Janet Knott USA
*Space shuttle Challenger explodes
seconds after launching at
Cape Canaveral, Florida*

1987 Anthony Suau USA
*South Korean woman after her son has
been arrested by riot police at a student
demonstration against election fraud*

1988 Ramazan Öztürk TURKEY
*Victims of Iraqi army's chemical weapons
attack on a Kurdish villag*

1989 Anthony Suau USA
*West German man with
a hammer at the Berlin Wall*

1990 Therese Frare USA
*AIDS patient David Kirby dies
in the company of his family*

1991 Kenneth Jarecke USA
*Body of Iraqi soldier after allied
forces bombing in the Gulf War*

1992 Luc Delahaye FRANCE
*People seek shelter from shelling
and gunfire in Sarajevo*

1993 Larry Towell CANADA
Palestinian boys with toy guns in Gaza City

1994 James Nachtwey USA
*Mutilated Hutu man at a Red Cross
Hospital in Rwanda*

1955

-1995

COVER CAPTIONS

1982